THE SECRETS OF MANIPULATION:

BECOME A MASTER IN DARK PSYCOLOGY, PERSUASION, MIND CONTROL AND TRY TO INFLUENCE PEOPLE WITH EMPATH, COVER NLP TECHNIQUES AND SKILLS TO GOOD RELATIONSHIPS.

contained within this document, including, but not limited to, —
errors, omissions, or inaccuracies.

Table of Contents

Description

Introduction

Chapter 1 Traits of Manipulators

Chapter 2 Signs of Mental Manipulation to Look For

Chapter 3 How to instantly recognize a mind manipulator in your love relationship

Chapter 4 Neuro-Linguistic Programming and Manipulation

Chapter 5 How to Manipulate People Psychologically and How to Lie

Chapter 6 Mind Control

Chapter 7 Effective Communication and how to Enhance Your Social Skills

Chapter 8 Tone and Pitch – Where Verbal meets Non-verbal

Chapter 9 How to Improve Your Positivity

Chapter 10 The Most Powerful Mind-Power Tool

Chapter 11 Persuading Someone with Your Words

Chapter 12 Non-Verbal Communication

Chapter 13 Stop Manipulation

Chapter 14 Tips for Safeguarding Yourself from Manipulation

Conclusion

Description

The world today is full of different manipulations. Everywhere you go, all around you, someone or some company is trying their best to persuade you one way or another. Most people don't realize that they could be falling victim to a manipulator when they buy things, go places, or even when you feel as if you're doing something nice for someone. Different ads try to create emotion within you, while commercials intentionally attempt to plant ideas as if you've had them yourself. You could just as easily experience manipulation between the people you meet, or already know. The worst of these, is when the manipulation comes from someone that you know and care about.

Truth be told, this isn't a new art form that we've learned about this century. The art of manipulation goes back long before we ever began recording history. Manipulation has been prevalent for as long as the concept of power has been around. Interesting enough, the further away from an event we get, the more we find it manipulated altogether. Your memory fails within certain realms, and is replaced by falsified memories from someone else, or maybe even from yourself. That makes it difficult to pinpoint specifics of manipulation throughout history, due to the events themselves being tweaked, though you'll always find traces throughout time, wherever you look. Manipulation is also used as an important plot device in your favorite TV shows and novels. Take the ever so popular Game of Thrones for instance.

There are many people that try to use their position of power or their might to allow them wins towards the Iron Throne, but it's the cunning ones, the ones who have mastered manipulation, who still stand tall all the end to the end.

This guide will focus on the following:

- Traits of Manipulators
- Signs of Mental Manipulation to Look For
- Neuro-Linguistic Programming and Manipulation
- How to Manipulate People Psychologically and How to Lie
- Mind Control
- How to Improve Your Positivity
- The Most Powerful Mind-Power Tool
- Persuading Someone with Your Words
- Non-Verbal Communication
- Stop Manipulation... AND MORE!!!

Introduction

One of the most common words you'll see when it comes to understanding manipulation is "Influence". Either you're being influenced to do something that maybe you weren't too keen on doing in the first place, or the reverse, you could be attempting to influence someone else. This influence usually comes from subtle nuances, and indirect psychological maneuvers, so that the person in question doesn't even realize they've been manipulated most of the time. Because of this, manipulation is traditionally seen as devious, and is only looking to benefit the interest of the manipulator.

Manipulation can wear many faces, so that usually you're unaware of any techniques being applies on you at all. As an example, you have a friend who is a single parent, and she's been raving about a date she has this Friday night. The closer it gets to Friday, the more excited she seems about it. The day before Friday she comes to you in tears, her ex has cancelled on taking care of their daughter, leaving your friend without a sitter for Friday night. Although you've already told her about your own plans, your friend proceeds to ask you about babysitting. You decline, but she persists, insisting she's been looking forward to this date for a while. Again, you decline, and still she persists, now claiming that if you were a good friend then you'd do it. Are you being manipulated?

A second example involves you working hard to reach a deadline with your team. Even though everyone is working hard, it doesn't seem like you're going to be able to make your deadline by the end of the day. As the clock strikes five, you and your co-workers clean up, knowing you'll have to try again tomorrow. However, your boss walks up to you, and asks if you can stay later to finish any work that hadn't gotten done during the day. You inform him about your dinner plans, and that unfortunately you won't be able to stay. That's when he makes a comment about your work ethic, and a possible promotion that would only go to someone that showed they were there for the company. You do want that promotion, despite your dinner plans. Are you being manipulated?

In both examples, yes, you're being manipulated.

In our first example, your friend is trying to guilt you into feeling bad, while she escapes from her responsibilities. Even the nicest person has their own tasks to complete and can't always go out of their way to help a friend. Even though you've already said no, your friend has continued to badger you about it, trying to wear you down. Lastly, she's trying to leverage your friendship in order to manipulate your behavior, which, is not a very good friend. In our second example, our boss is trying to dangle a promotion over us without saying it. On one hand, you're pretty sure he's trying to tell you that you'll receive the job promotion if you stay, whereas if you don't, the promotion could go to someone else. However, your boss never technically promised you anything, and if you stay the extra time, there's nothing holding him to your expectation of receiving a promotion. This leaves you in an awkward position of having to cave to your boss, for fear of retaliation.

As we continue, you'll not only gain a firm grip of understanding, but your eyes will also be opened to the entirety of manipulation. The curtain will be peeled back, and you'll uncover a whole new world, much larger than you previously thought possible. The average person who skims on the top of manipulation, what it fully entails, and what can be accomplished. As you learn techniques, you'll also learn how to further protect yourself, because while there is such a thing as positive manipulation, the other side also exists.

Chapter 1 Traits of Manipulators

A "sheep in wolves clothing" is often the analogy used to describe those who would use manipulation for their own personal gain. While that's not always the case, there are some typical traits of manipulative people to watch out for.

For one, a manipulator tends to be incredibly short-sighted. They're unable to see past what's directly in front of them and have a very difficult time trying to plan their next moves. This is because a manipulator tends to be only focused on their own goals and can't see past what they need for themselves. They're so fixed upon the goal that's in front of them, they can't see beyond that point. This also means that when the opposite is explained to them, they can't comprehend. The idea doesn't benefit them in any way, so they can't seem to see it. Furthermore, they don't question themselves one bit, and never see themselves as having any issues. Instead, anyone else is considered the problem and they typically can't be swayed one way or another even if they are in the wrong.

Most manipulators also don't understand the concept of boundaries. They tend to crowd around you, whether that be physically, emotionally, or psychologically. This is because a manipulator lacks understanding on identity and personal space. They'll continue to burst through your personal bubble at any time they feel. Not only do they not understand the concept, but they also feel it as a form of control. If they are constantly in your personal space, they are always the one seen with the power in any situation. It's difficult to regain control with another person when they've crowded around your space without any qualms about it. Manipulators test social rules all the time, and their favorite thing is to break them. This displays a sense of dominance that most manipulators are drawn towards. The only action that would cause them to back down is being vocal about your boundaries. Even then, this will often cause a display of bravado that puts blame back onto you for being offended in the first place.

Another side effect of their lack of boundaries, is their ability to become incredibly clingy. Because of this, the manipulator acts as a sort of parasite, feeding off another's energy and positivity. This constant interaction and disregard of boundaries depletes the opposite individual, while the manipulator moves on to the next person.

Typically, a trait of a successful manipulator is that they are a master wordsmith. Their actions don't match up evenly with what they say, and of course when they're called out on it, they become hostile. Most of the time, nobody even realizes this because the manipulator is so good about twisting and turning words. They can get away with almost anything, simply by talking their way out of it. Even if they end up talking in circles, most people don't realize that the manipulator isn't even making sense. Because they continue speaking, usually with a passionate tone, it gives off the illusion that they must know what they're speaking about. In truth, a manipulator is just gifted with words and gab, so even when they find themselves in a bit of a jam and don't what they're doing. They someone make it out scathed regardless.

One of the strongest traits of a manipulator is that they are people users. There's no doubt about it, the main purpose of a manipulator is to get other people to do what they want. Because of this, they never really develop a since of caring for other people in their life. Often, you'll find them taking advantage of each and every person they possibly can. The way this begins is a manipulator spotting someone with multiple good qualities about them. These qualities usually include one or a combination of kindness and humility. At first, these qualities are expressed as something they can praise you for, and make you feel good. You'll be told what a wonderful person you are, only for them to turn around and diminish these traits later. Manipulators don't care about you or learning anything about you, all they care about is what you can do for them. Manipulators use people like pieces of garbage, always to be thrown away once they're done using them. Because of this, manipulators can never maintain friendships, constantly stuck in this cycle of using others until they're spent.

A well-rounded person probably has certain topics that they are passionate about and hold opinions towards. However, it's natural to change those ideas and opinions within the presence of new information. It's not the most fun to admit when you're wrong, but most people know that nobody can be perfect. The manipulator tends to hold strong beliefs, that are seemingly unchangeable. Even if they are presented with new information that could discredit their argument, the manipulator will hold this belief true, simply so that they're not seen as wrong. Giving up this bit, would give up control in their mind, and we know by now that manipulators love to be in control. If anything, their new goal becomes to change your belief. Better yet, to be able to control their belief. This is why you'll find many manipulators become crusaders for topics that may not be considered socially important, or even for false reasons altogether.

Everyone wants to hear the hot gossip, but a manipulator, is always going to be the one gossiping. Manipulators are good at getting others to spill their secrets, but you won't often find them keeping those secrets. They'll be the first to whisper into the darkness about one of their friends. This is also a good way to know whether or not your friend is gossiping about you, because if they're coming to you with secrets belonging to others, you're probably being talked about behind your back, as well. Manipulators are masters at triangulation using people, pitting people against one another. Their goal is to create rivals between people, create entertainment for themselves, as they watch from the sidelines as if they had no hand in anything. They also tend to be the same people who refuse to choose a side, but have secretly expressed to the dueling parties how they agree with them. This makes the manipulator comes off as the good guy, a true friend, in the situation, even if they were the person who caused it.

Manipulators can't seem to understand you, nor the reasons you do things. Self-disclosure is a tough thing, but it's needed in order to divulge more and more of yourself within friendships and relationships. It allows for the other person to see the real you, and to accept you as you are. However, manipulators don't understand you, no matter how hard they appear to be trying. The truth is, they have their heart on misunderstanding you, because they aren't really trying. They may be experts at pretending like they are, but at the end of the day they simply do not care. Don't waste your time on explaining who you are to them, because you're only going to end up disappointed. Remember, the manipulator isn't interested in you as a person, they're interested in what you can do for them. This can cause a sense of guilt to develop within you, after giving so much of yourself to someone and allowing you to see them in that light.

A common advice is to ask yourself if the person in question remembers personal things about you. Possibly something a little more than your birthday or favorite color, but important facts this person should be able to remember. If not, then do yourself a favor and access what it is you want in a true friendship or relationship. They may attempt to brush it off as a lapse in memory, and if you persist, they'll try to spin it back around on you as if you're overreacting. It's imperative you remember what's important to you.

Naturally, a talented manipulator is going to be able to hide some of these traits, especially if they believe that you may have purchased a book to assist you. Looking for these specific traits within someone may not yield the same results as being able to see it in action. Again, manipulators are going to hide their true intentions no matter what, so there's no sense in believing they wouldn't try to mask anything else in their lives. Although it will help immensely, simply knowing the traits of a manipulator will not give you the power to point one out in the crowd. It'll take much more than that, but luckily, we're going to cover several topics that can help.

Chapter 2 Signs of Mental Manipulation to Look For

When you're in the middle of a manipulative situation, it can be hard to see the woods for the trees, however, it's worthwhile being aware of the signs of mental manipulation, so you can attempt to extract yourself from a damaging situation. It's also good to know these in case you can see someone else being manipulated. Whilst it's hard to convince someone that manipulation is a part of their life, by pointing out the signs you're doing enough to make them question the situation, and that could be enough to open their eyes.

The main signs of mental manipulation include:

You're Constantly Hearing Lies When You Know The Truth

If someone is telling you they didn't say something or didn't do something, but you know that they did, that's a big red flag. For instance, a partner might tell you they're going out to see their brother, but you happen to bump into their brother in the street and they tell you they never saw them. When you mention this to your partner they tell you that they never said that, they told you they were going to see a friend. It might seem possible, in fact, it is, but it's also quite likely to be a lie. When this is a constant thing, i.e. it's happening a lot and you know you're not wrong, it's a real possibility that this person is manipulating you into believing what they want you to believe, and not what you know to be true.

What They Say And What They Do Are Two Different Things

We've said this a few times already, but always watch actions and don't pay too much attention to words. A person who is manipulating you will tell you exactly what they know you want to hear. For instance, if your partner stays out all night and you suspect they were with someone else, of course, you don't want to hear that they were, you want them to tell you they fell asleep at their cousin's house after watching a film. They know this, and they will tell you this, giving you relief from your anguish. The problem is, they're more likely to have been doing the thing you fear.

It's also likely that a manipulator will promise you the Earth and never give it to you, always disappointing you and letting you down. When you question them on this, they will turn it around on you and make you seem like the unreasonable one, telling you how lucky you are to have them and you don't appreciate them, perhaps. You then start to feel guilty for questioning them, questioning your sanity, and backing down. This will happen again and again, on loop.

They Are Masters at Guilt Tricks

Whenever you mention something they have done wrong or something which is upsetting you, they will turn the whole situation around and make it your fault. They might get upset themselves, cry, get angry, throw something, or question why you're bringing it up. You then feel guilty for even mentioning it, wishing you'd kept quiet, telling yourself that it wasn't a big deal, and kicking yourself for not keeping your mouth shut. This is manipulation to let them get away with whatever they want to do, without any ramifications for their actions.

Everything is Someone Else's Fault - Usually Yours

A manipulator cannot take responsibility for their actions, especially if they are narcissistic. Everything can be blamed on someone else, and most of the time that will be you. A manipulator is fantastic at playing the victim and they have no grasp on consequences for actions. Again, this means they can get away with absolutely anything because they will simply blame it on another person and use their clever words to make you believe it.

They Make You Responsible For Their Moods

If a manipulator is angry, it's your job to fix it; if a manipulator is sad, you have to solve the problem; if a manipulator is happy, you'll simply be glad that there is no major turmoil going on right at that moment. A manipulator makes the victim responsible for every single one of their moods and when it's a negative mood, every single person in that room will know about it. They can't just get on with their day, knowing that they're having a bad one and assuming it will pass, it's far more likely to be a catastrophic mood that everyone has to feel and be sucked into.

Again, this is an extremely narcissistic trait, but it's one that many manipulators will exhibit too. If you're constantly up and down, at the mercy of the manipulator's moods, that's a red flag coming your way.

They Always go One Better Than You

If you have a headache, they have a migraine; if you're hungry, they're starving; if you're tired, they're exhausted. A manipulator will always go one better and make everything about them. Again, we're talking narcissists here. The bottom line is that they are saying something deeper, on a non-verbal level; they're telling you that their needs and problems are far worse than yours, so you need to focus on them and stop complaining about your own. Of course, this isn't the truth at all, but their behavior forces you to think that way. In the end, you might simply stop verbalizing your own needs, because you know theirs will always take precedence.

They Use Your Weaknesses Against You

A manipulator will go to great effort to find out your weaknesses and your vulnerabilities. When they find these out, they will use them against you, pushing your buttons and causing you emotional turmoil. Of course, they'll then be the ones to catch you when you're having a meltdown, which is enough to make you question whether or not you heard what you heard, saw what you did, etc. This is a gaslighting technique which is unfortunately very successful and keeps the victim off-kilter, not really sure what to believe.

If you're noticing these tactics with someone in your life, perhaps it's time to sit up and take notice. Of course, in order for this to add up to true manipulation, there needs to be ticking off boxes on a regular basis. It can be that you notice someone we've just mentioned only once and never again; that's simply a human being making a mistake. On the other hand, if you notice that someone is using one of these tactics, or even more than one, and it's a regular thing, you might very well have a manipulator in your life.

Chapter 3 How to instantly recognize a mind manipulator in your love relationship

Many people can sense when there is something unusual in their relationship. However, very few will actually give a name to the issue and sort it out. For instance, a person may notice that the partner is too controlling and wants everything done his/her way. Instead of acknowledging that he/she might be dealing with a manipulator, this person will continuously make excuses for the partner until things get out of hand.

The feeling of being emotionally manipulated is very unpleasant-And if you are on the lookout, it is easy to recognize it immediately. However, you might not understand how it is being done at that moment. In fact, it can be hard for you to rely on your own judgment when the truths and facts are being twisted by the manipulator. It is therefore important to know how manipulation happens and what you should look out for in a relationship. If you realize that your partner has been manipulating you all along, do not get angry- it will be just as important to understand why he/she uses manipulation techniques.

First thing y9ou might notice in manipulator is that he/she oversimplifies things. For instance, if you have done something seemingly inappropriate, regardless of your reasons or the complications in the situation that lead there, this person might say "I would never do that no matter what. " In simple terms, this person is putting the situation in black and white- " What you did was wrong and there is no reason good enough to justify it." You will give the most sincere reason and still that person will disqualify you. Owe unto you if you disagree with their judgment- they classify you as totally unreasonable. No interpretation will be considered, no explanation will be acknowledged. You were wrong and that's final. If you sense this in your relationship, then you are being manipulated.

Secondly, a manipulative partner will focus on the point of argument that favors them. No matter what you say, this person will refocus your point in a way that favors him/her. Circumstances will be turned around to your disadvantage. You will hear something like " I would never do that to you". This person will ignore the complexity of the situation. In a manipulator's language, you will realize an overgeneralization- the use of words such as never, and always. This makes the point seem like the rule-which then oversimplifies things-into 'good' and 'bad' category. Emotionally, the emotions you will feel in such an argument can be overwhelming thus making you to either concede defeat or apologies.

Thirdly, look out for exaggerated language- manipulative partners tend to use it. For instance, if you ask the manipulative person to do something twice, he/she might call it 'harassment' or 'abuse'. This might be something as simple as telling the person to pick some groceries in the store on the way home. A manipulative person will imbue an ambiguous gesture or event with a meaning that seems impossible to argue with. For instance, you might forget to switch off the lights and this person will say that you are only looking for ways to add on to the current bills. A casual remark may be magnified into a monstrous character flaw.

You will also notice that a manipulative partner will overstate his/her exemptions when engaging in an argument. You might hear something like " I have hit the bottom. Can't you see the pain you are causing me? " Most events will be construed in a way that emphasizes the depth of pain and suffering you have brought upon the person. The intention here is to extract more concessions from you. Furthermore, the manipulator will thrive on making you feel guilty and do whatever he/she wants. For instance, " I am feeling so hurt today. Can you please do... for me?" Even if you had your own issues, chances are, you will stop talking about them and help this person.

You will also notice that this person does not offer you any help when you have a problem, instead, he/she will make everything about them. For instance, you might explain how rough your day at the office was and this partner will say "That was nothing compared to mine. It was even worse and I am not complaining about it." In simple terms, his person is telling you to not be such a 'whiny baby'.

The character of manipulative people suggests that they are projecting their issues onto the world. They are simply finding evidence to support their preconceptions and viewing life in the lens of their own happiness. The defensive stances they often take are used to evade responsibility for their own behavior. These kinds of partners will agree to something then later deny it. If you engage in an argument with them and seem to be winning, they instantly change the topic into something you cannot refute. A manipulative partner will even bring unrelated concepts to an argument just so that he/she can confuse or destabilize you and win. Overall, you will always be on edge when dealing with this person simply because he/she is somehow unstable. You never know what is going to set them off next.

Such characters indicate that the manipulator is insecure and would rather not choose a side or take responsibility for anything. As you start putting these characteristics into place, it will be easy to see that the manipulator does not always act out of malice. Sometimes it is because of emotional deregulation, combined with dysfunctional coping skills. Manipulative people are in most cases trying to express their hurt, confusion, and fears. The main challenge with them is that they do not know how to reach out for help. The need to hide those weaknesses is too great. So, instead of apologizing for a mistake, they will attack you and take a defensive stand. It is easier to pass the blame to someone else than take responsibility.

Besides, these manipulators are not happy with the sadness brewing inside them and are unable to deal with it. This is truer for people dealing with a borderline personality disorder which is a condition where the affected person experiences extreme disruptions in his/her sense of self. His/her close relations suffer due to this disorder. A person suffering from this condition may feel an extreme and deep-rooted need to be loved and accepted. However, these needs will still be affected by the normal challenges experienced in relationships and this p3erson does not know how to tackle them. Consequently, the person will develop a kind of over-reactivity and hypersensitivity, emotionally, forcing him/her to revert to primitive defense mechanisms, such as denial.

Because the person is unable to meet the deep need for love and acceptance or any other feeling he/she craves for, he/she will resort to manipulative behaviors as described above. Although it is not every person with conditions that might lead to manipulative behavior (such as Borderline Personality Disorder) exhibit these characteristics, it is important to understand that some of the cases involving manipulations are not all about control. Some of these manipulators are just making a silent and hidden cry for help.

It is important to consider if that manipulative partner is just selfish or he/she is making a cry for help. If there is a condition that is making him/her be manipulative, then seek help- such as medical treatment and counseling. On the other hand, if the partner is just being mean for no good reason, it might be time for you to leave. If you support a manipulative partner and request him/her to make the necessary changes, then he/she fails to do so; you need to look for your own peace of mind, even if you have to walk away.

The difference between love and manipulation

In the world today, there is new information about love and relationships coming up every day. In the morning, you will read an article about how to attract a spouse and in the afternoon there will be another new piece of information about who is single again. After two hours, you will see another article on 'how to know if he/she loves you' and there will be endless pieces of information put together to make life look a little simpler than reality.

After reading most of these articles and paying attention to the advice given, one might be tempted to think that he/she has all it takes to start and retain a long term relationship. However, it is important to understand that a love relationship involves two people and no matter how willing you are to be a good partner, you cannot have a perfect relationship on your own. YORU partner has to be willing too.

We all hope to find a long term partner-b someone to share our lives with. The internet and social media have made love look so appealing and easy. Love gives us hope- for a better tomorrow, and we need a lot of that. The thought of a lasting relationship makes it all seem so worth it. However, there is a risk of faking in love with the wrong person. If you get into a relationship with the wrong person, life might become very rough. Interestingly, people stay in wrong relationships because there is hope for tomorrow- maybe the person will change. In the process, a person finds him/herself stuck with a manipulative partner.

How can one tell the difference between manipulation and Love? There are some obvious and not so obvious indicators of manipulation in a relationship. For instance, when you are with a manipulative partner, you will feel confused. But when you are with a person who truly loves you, then most of the things are clear and there is no hypocrisy.

Healthy love is built on honesty while manipulative love is hypocritical

If your partner truly loves you, he/she will be honest. This person will want the relationship to last therefore will use integrity when handling relationship matters. Healthy love involves telling each other the truth even when it hurts. There is no passive-aggressive behavior in this relationship. You will realize there is empathy, thus everyone opens up. The level of understanding in this relationship allows for every individual to open up. Even feedbacks are taken positively because they are explained without judgment or unnecessary harshness. A healthy relationship will inspire the two people involved to change and become better for each other.

On the other hand, an unhealthy relationship will keep the spouses on edge because of the plaid rules placed upon each other. Normally, the manipulative partner makes unnecessary and illogical demands on the subject. Interestingly, this manipulator will not live by the same stands and when confronted, he/she becomes defensive and projects all the issues to the other partner.

Healthy love will find humor but a manipulative one will involve nitpicking.

A person who truly loves another will see them as human, therefore, leave room for errors. In every relationship, there is something that partners find irritating about each other. How the two people choose to handle these issues is the determinant of success or failure. In a healthy relationship. The spouses will find ways to overlook, tolerate and gradually change the weakness of each other. They will focus on the bigger picture and make each other to feel accepted as they are.

However, people in unhealthy relationships will focus on such idiosyncrasies regardless of the size, then blow them out of proportion. The manipulative partner will find fault in every situation and make it a big deal. For instance if a person is late by three minutes, the manipulator will complain about it the whole day and even insinuate that the other person is lazy and always late even though that is not the case. A manipulative partner will not leave room for growth or change- and will consistently change the goalposts.

Those partners who focus on nitty-gritty will have strict rules on matters such as eating habits, chores, cleanliness, timekeeping, and other dismissible matters. You might be tempted to think that the people who focus on such matters are intelligent and awesome but that is not always the case. In a relationship, if one person pays too much attention to these small matters, it might become hard to attend to bigger issues. If such nitty grits are the determinants of respect in the relationship, it might be unhealthy. Does not over-focus on the small matters, instead, leave room for the big ones. Rigidity will kill your relationship.

Manipulators have hidden self-centered agendas while healthy love focuses on building the relationship.

One major reason why people fail to recognize manipulator is infatuation- that blinding passion and admiration. There is always the risk of admiring someone too much especially in the initial stages of a relationship thus ignoring the warning signs.

That flame-like feeling can make one not to identify a manipulator. As such, we stay in a relationship thinking it is love, only to realize later that the other person had a selfish agenda. And BOOM- the heartbreak.

In a healthy relationship, the spouses do not look for ways to control each other, rather, they built each other up. True love will be open and flexible meaning, no one will force the other into doing things. The level of trust in a healthy relationship will allow everyone to comfortably choose what they want, to be real and also comfortable.

Sadly, an unhealthy and manipulative relationship is about who has power over the other- who is in charge- and who gets what. One person feels more important than the other. The relationship is not a balanced give and take. One person is always giving while the other is every taking and giving nothing in return. Everything flows to one side. The strength of love is measured by what one person does for the other.

True love compliments whereas manipulators use insults and intimidation.

A healthy love will be about empowering each other. The partners will look for the good in each other and bring it out. There is a lot of physical emotional and verbal acknowledgment. A healthy love will be offer support, clear communication and nurturing. The people involved will encourage each other to live their dreams. If there is some form of failure, the partners will lift each other up.

Unlike healthy relationships, manipulative ones will do not empower. The manipulative partner does not enjoy the success of the other because he/she is afraid of losing him/her. As such, the manipulative person will look for ways to belittle the other and facilitate their failure. In fact, he/she will somehow relish the failure of the other person and even say, 'I told you so' when things do not work out as expected.

Manipulators fear the independence of the subject, therefore, will withhold any support they can offer. This lack of support is it physical or emotional, will ensure that the person stays dependent on the manipulative person and thus give him/her the opportunity to continue using the victim. The victim will not be courageous enough to leave because he/she does not want to lose that support.

Healthy love allows for disagreements while manipulation involves fighting

Researches show that all couple disagrees but the difference is how the people involve handling their matters. When two people have a healthy love, it becomes easy to move on after a disagreement. Misunderstandings are not taken as determinants of life or death. Differences in opinions are not the highlight of true love, neither are they a source of blame. The partners focus on finding common ground and moving on positively. Everyone was born and raised in different environments under different conditions thus, we cannot be similar in every aspect. The beauty of life is in our diversity. Can you imagine how boring life would be if we all agreed on everything?

Being in a relationship does not mean that people agree on everything. In fact, that would make such a boring relationship. Healthy love will encourage diversity as it is the opportunity to grow.

However, if spouses lack an understanding, diversity will be a hindrance of success. A manipulative partner believes in 'My way or the highway. Selfish partners cannot agree to disagree and move on, instead, they will dwell on the matter at hand and even blow things out of proportion. Every argument will be taken personally thus destroying the relationship. Every differing pinion is a platform for another fight, a chance to belittle the other- an opportunity to proof each other wrong.

A small matter will become full-blown arguments accompanied by silent treatment until one person gives in and apologizes. Normally, the passive partner gives in and allows the other to win in order to avoid further conflict. He/she fails to realize that a giving in only empowers the manipulator to keep blowing things up.

Genuine love is positive whereas manipulation stares on the downside

When there is true love in your relationship, you will not strain excessively to keep things in order. You will not have to go completely out of your way to keep the other person happy. Love is fun, open, easy, relaxed, and active. And peaceful. Basically, every partner will know his/her role in the relationship. As such, he/she will ensure that the other is not hurt and the rare cases where there might be misunderstandings, apologies will come easily. In a genuine relationship, a partner will watch his/her actions, feedbacks and feelings to avoid stepping on the feelings of the other.

The types of emotions, attitudes, and efforts brought into a relationship determine the direction of the relationship. If anyone of the partners decides to be manipulative, that relationship will come to a halt, sooner or later. In lasting and healthy relationships, the partners consciously choose to pay attention to the strengths and look for ways to positively handle the weaknesses in each other. Focusing on the positive side of a person makes it easy to love him/her. On the other side, paying attention to weaknesses makes it very hard to love or even tolerate the person.

Manipulative relationships are the exact opposite of healthy relationships. The partners focus on the downsides of each other. The manipulative spouse will always point out the things that are wrong in the other person. Every time a small mistake occurs, the manipulator will create a world war IV out of it. There is literally no room for human errors in manipulative relationships because one person will use the mistakes as leverage. The amount of bashing in that relationship is unbearable to any normal person. The consequences of this manipulation are immense, starting from hurt, division and even hate. The connection in that relationship will be largely based on of feelings hates and despise.

Genuine love offers freedom while manipulative relationships thrive on control

Love is protective but not controlling. We often mistake the two terms in relationships. Love will not limit your space- if anything, it will facilitate freedom. Everyone needs their space even when in a relationship. A healthy relationship should encourage growth through freedom, more so freedom of thought and expression. The only way to maintain a lasting relationship is through allowing each other to be free- express one without imitations. A healthy love relationship will leave you room to be happy outside the relationship. You will comfortably have friends outside the relationship and your spouse will hardly try to control your choice of who to keep close or otherwise. However, a caring partner may give you an opinion on one or two things but not force you to take their choice. For instance, your partner may give you a bit of honest advice about a friend you keep but he/she will not force you to cut the communication.

On the other side, manipulative relationships cut off your freedom. You will not be allowed to have friends or a life outside a stipulated circle set by the manipulator. Basically, the manipulator is afraid of giving you freedom because he/she knows you might discover what you deserve and leave them. In unhealthy relationships, the controlling partner does not allow the other to participate in activities outside the relationship. He/she ensures that the victim depends on him/her only. Manipulators may even go to the extent of cutting the communication between you and your family so that you have no one to build you. One dark manipulation skill that has been found to be very effective is Isolation. It is more of a divide and rule concept whereby, it is easy to manipulate one person around compared to a group. Isolation in the manipulative relationship makes sure that the victim depends on the manipulator and slowly the two will be toxic to each other.

Healthy love is clear but manipulative relationships are confusing

Have you ever been in a relationship where you could not really tell what was happening? It was more like you were walking on eggshells the whole time because your partner could be happy for one minute and then exploding with anger in the next? That partner might have been a manipulator.

If you want to know if your relationship is healthy or unhealthy, ask yourself, "do I feel confused in this relationship, or can I see everything clearly?" Are you sure of where you stand or do you have to keep guessing? A confusing relationship will gradually mess with your inner peace. In fact, there will come a time when you will feel lost in the relationship. That relationship will hardly survive.

On the other hand, partners in healthy relationships will hold nothing back. Everything is clear and anyone can express him/herself without fear of judgment. Because of this openness, the partners do not allow things to pill up.

Healthy and genuine love leads to a strong and fun relationship where the partners want to spend a lot of time together. Opposing, unhealthy love drives the partners apart because they are so consumed with controlling rather than building each other. If it is evident that the person you will meet at home in the evening is self-centered, chances are, you will avoid going there. If you know that your opinion will be blasted by that manipulative partner, chances are, you will reserve it for yourself. Instead of spending your energy on constructive healthy relationship issues, you will focus on avoiding misunderstandings.

Anyone who has ever been in a manipulative relationship knows how devastating it can be thus he/she appreciates a healthy relationship. It is possible to have a healthy relationship based on true love rather than manipulation. However, this kind of relationships can only be experienced by two people who consciously choose to use grace, integrity, and Honesty while handling their matters. If you want a healthy relationship, it is important to be careful when choosing who to love. Look for someone who shares your dreams and wants to have a lasting relationship. Before you commit yourself, look out for signs of manipulation such as self-centered agendas. A person who truly loves and cares for you will maintain a healthy level of respect in the relationship. He/she will not push you to make a rushed decision.

Chapter 4 Neuro-Linguistic Programming and Manipulation

NLP or Neuro Linguistic Programming is one of today's most widely used mind control, persuasion, manipulation and influencing techniques. It is applied by everyone from salespersons to political leaders to media bigwigs.

The method was invented by John Grinder and Richard Bandler in the 70s, and its popularity spiraled in the world of marketing, public relations, advertising, sales and even personal/social relationships. People who master NLP are known to be equipped with the ability to trick people into doing whatever they want them to in several incredible ways.

The duo Bandler and Grinder came up with a sort of new age version of hypnotherapy. While conventional hypnosis is dependent upon putting the subject or client into a state of trance, NLP isn't as heavily loaded. It is about layering or planting suggestions into the subject's unconscious mind through the clever use of language or semantics, without them knowing that you are using the technique.

Today the strategies of NLP and hypnotic writing are widely used in the internet marketing, social media and make money online scams. The sales copy of most get rich quick schemes is cleverly worded to manipulate the unsuspecting reader into taking the intended action.

People trained in the art of NLP are experts in watching out for eye movements, pupil dilation, flush of the skin and other neurologically linked signals that reveal plenty about the person's thought process.

For instance, simply by observing a person an NLP trained person can determine what side of the brain is dominantly used by the individual.

They can also identify what sense (sight, hearing, smell, etc.) is most powerful in the person. The manner in which the brain organizes, stores and uses information (can be determined through a person's eye movements) and when they are giving false information or making stories.

For example, an individual who is primarily focused on seeing will use words and phrases that hold visual metaphors such as, "Do you really see my point?" Similarly, a person is more focused on hearing with tend to use "Hear me" or "I hear you." This is the language that you should stick to as a manipulator trying to get them to do what you want. You'll score higher points with a visual person by using words such as "look at the situation in this way." It is all about wording your talks in a way that plays on their linguistic programming.

By mirroring a person's body language and specific linguistic patterns, the manipulator is aiming to build a rapport. It is a psychological process where a person lets their guard down and arrives at the conclusion that the manipulator or NLPer is similar to them or like them. What the NLPer does is fakes certain social clues that lead a person to drop the defenses they build around themselves for other people (especially strangers). This makes them more open and receptive to any suggestions that the NLPer plans to embed in their mind.

NLP helps the manipulator train others into thinking and doing what they want. It is about influencing the subject's thoughts, feelings, and behavior in a way that is beneficial for the manipulator. Skilled manipulators know how to use the power of anchors (external influences) for sparking or triggering specific emotions in people. For instance, a song that is associated with the subject's first kiss can be used for triggering all emotions related to that moment.

Do not we all experience this in everyday life? Certain songs remind us of particular moments or phases in our life and hence become associated with the emotions we felt during those moments or phases. Each time we hear those songs, our subconscious experiences the same feelings and emotions. The song in this example acts as the emotional anchor to help induce feelings and emotions that you want in the other person.

Let's take another example. Each time a person buys coffee for you, you talk about something pleasant that happened in his or her life like his or her marriage or the birth of his child. If you talk about the birth of his or her child consistently every time the person buys you coffee, they will come to associate buying coffee for you with pleasant, positive emotions. It acts as a sort of anchor for his or her feelings.

NLP is a complex discipline that cannot be acquired in a day. It needs hours and hours of practice with reading people's subconscious behavior, understanding their neurological programming and more. However, as beginner manipulator, you'd want to understand some popular techniques used by NLPers on their subjects.

Here are a few expert techniques NLPers use to manipulate people or control their minds.

1. They Observe Eye Movements

NLPers will always closely observe their subject's eye movements to determine what part of the brain is being used, and how the subject stores/uses information. They give the impression that they are keenly interested in what the other person is saying and actually care about knowing their thoughts when in reality they are simply analyzing how a person access information from different parts of his or her brain.

Within a few minutes, practitioners of NLP can tell if a person is lying or telling the truth. The subject will almost end up believing that the manipulator has some psychic abilities or telepathic superpowers. NLPers carefully calibrate eye movements to know conclude which parts of a brain are most active in a person, and how they process information.

2. Use the Power of Touch

NLPers use the power of touch effectively to induce certain feelings and emotions in their subjects without the subject even realizing it. Let us say for instance that the subject is in a particular state of emotion such as happy, angry, upset, sad, etc., NLP practitioners will use touch (light tap on the subject's shoulder or touch their arm) and anchor that particular form of touch by linking it to a specific emotion.

Each time you want to invoke that specific emotion in a person to fulfill your intent, simply use the particular touch that you did when the subject was experiencing the same emotion earlier.

3. Use Vague Words and Phrases

One of the fundamental methods of NLP is the generous use of vague verbiage for inducing a sort of hypnotic trance on the subject. NLPers believe that the more ambiguous and vaguer your language, the less likely is to your subject to opposing your ideas or disagree with you, thus making it easier to lead them into the trance state. You are basically limiting their ability to react to what you are saying.

Did you notice how effectively former United States of America President Barrack Obama used this technique during the famous "change campaign?" It was a word wrought in complete ambiguity. Anyone could interpret it in a way they wanted.

4. Relaxed and Permissive Words

Expert NLP hypnotists never start by telling their subjects what they want them to do outright. The commands follow more permissive and relaxed issuances such as "please feel free to de-stress or relax" or "you can have this for as long as you like" or "you're welcome to test this product." The subject is sort of given a loose rope, and the impression that the NLPer really wants to relax and enjoy without restrictions.

The language use is more relaxing and permissive. Skilled hypnotists realize that this is more effective when it comes to driving the subject into a state of trance over immediately commanding them into it. When you begin with, "please feel free to let your hair down and relax completely", they are likelier to go into a trance gradually.

5. Layered Language

Skilled NLPers will always use language that is deeply layered or has hidden meaning/connotations attached to it. They'll use widely believed facts and slowly slip in their agenda into to manipulate the subject's subconscious mind into thinking in a particular way. For example, food, sleep and going outdoors with me are the formula for a healthy life.

On the surface of it, the subject's subconscious mind tends to agree with it because everyone has been conditioned to believe that food, sleep and getting fresh air is good for their health. They will tend to agree with it without giving it much thought. However, the layered message here is – going outdoors with me. And boy did you just get someone to agree to that on a subconscious level? This is an extremely subtle yet powerful NLP technique that is harnessed to the hilt by experienced NLP practitioners.

You also follow up one question with another to create what can be termed as a conditioning by association. For example, you ask someone, "How many fingers are there on the human hands?" followed quickly by "How many on ten hands?"

The answer to the first will be ten, while the answer to the second question most likely will be 100.

The first is, of course, right, while the second is wrong. The answer to the second is 50. As an NLPer, you are creating a trap for getting your subject to think the way you want to through careful conditioning through association.

In NLP, you essentially build anchors or baselines that you can lead your subjects to whenever you want. It can come to anyone with a little bit of training and practice.

Talking about the power of association, it is widely used by advertisers to manipulate consumers into associating certain products with specific attributes and lifestyles.

For instance, Coca-Cola always has these fancy advertisements about beautiful young people gulping glasses of bottles of the aerated beverage. They are hot (or cool if you please), rich, in gorgeous settings and look extremely cheerful. What are your impressions as you consume those images? That drinking Coca-Cola gives you access to the good life. The idea and associations are deeply installed and embedded in the subconscious mind and leads you to make a rather quick decision when it comes to purchasing.

6. Get them to Agree

If you can get your subjects to answer in the affirmative to several questions in a row, it will be tough for them to refuse your final request. NLPers know this only too well and use it liberally on their subjects to get them to do what they want.

This is one of the many clever manipulation and persuasion strategies used by sales and marketing folks. They will launch into a series of questions, the answer of which will rarely ever be in negative. After getting consecutive positive replies from their subjects, they will go for the kill and lead them into making impulsive and emotionally driven decisions. The entire technique is designed for engineering spur of the moment decisions by switching off the subject's ability to make logical decisions.

For example, an insurance salesperson will ask his client questions such as

"Wouldn't you like to financially secure the future of your loved ones?" Yes. "Wouldn't you like to use a policy that offers hassle-free claims?" Yes. "Wouldn't you want to protect your family's dream for a low as $123/month?" Yes. "Wouldn't you like your children's education and future dreams taken care of even when you aren't around?" Yes. "Wouldn't you want coverage for the immediate family under one policy at a single rate?" Yes.

"Then you should not waste any more time because you never know what happens in the next moment. Sign up for the policy immediately while it is available for a low monthly premium for a limited period."

See how a person is led into making a decision using the power of affirmatives or getting someone to agree to a series of questions before finally getting them to agree to the main thing. This can be as effective when you're asking someone out on a date.

When a person replies in the affirmative to a series of mostly emotional questions posed by the NLPer, it is hard for the subject to refuse the final offer.

7. Use Gibberish

NLP practitioners' resort to using a lot of gibberish mumbo-jumbo with the intention of attempting to program the subjects internal emotions and leading them into where the manipulator wants them to go. As an NLPer, you can't afford to be specific or explain precisely what you meant. You have to utilize trance invoking ambiguous language that throws the subject off gear and allows you to take complete control of their feelings and emotions.

Phrases such as, "As you let go of this emotion slowly, you will see yourself transitioning into a state of alignment with the aura of your success." It does not make any sense in the logical scheme of things, but your subject is befuddled into doing exactly what you want him or her to. Since it cannot be comprehended immediately, they'll be less prone to rejecting it in a state of confusion. When you do not know what to do or can't think for yourself, you are more susceptible to blindly following the instructions of the person who is guiding or leading you.

Chapter 5 How to Manipulate People Psychologically and How to Lie

A lot of people believe that manipulation is immoral and wrong. But sometimes it can even be used to achieve a positive outcome for both parties. Whatever your reason for manipulating people, here are the tactics to help horn your skills. For those who believe it's wrong, the following tactics give your ideas to know when you are being manipulated.

1. Lying by commission

It's never easy to know whether a person is lying when they are doing it, although often the truth may come out later when it is already too late. Understanding some personality types - especially that of psychopaths who are expert and frequent liars, who do it often in subtle ways, can go a long way in minimizing your chances of being lied to and manipulated.

Lying by the commission is when someone tells you something that is not a fact, or it is simply not true. Manipulators use this type of lie to twist the truth to create a version of something that happened, usually to favor themselves. A very simple example is when you know the weather outside is gloomy, but when asked, you just say, "Oh, it's perfectly sunny outside!" This way, the other person will make a decision to dress for sunny weather based on the wrong information they have been given.

This type of lie succeeds if the manipulated is willing to believe the lie, and the lie is also something that sounds plausible. Having a determination not to be lied to can go a long way in tackling this kind of lies. Always be skeptical about what you are being told and develop the habit of double-checking information.

2. Lying by omission

Let's say you have been dating your partner for quite some time then you come across the name Alice. You keep asking him "Who is Alice" and he would always change the topic immediately. But one day you press him for the truth, and he ends up telling you that he was once married to Alice for eight years. What might be disturbing isn't the fact that he was married but because he lied about it and it took you asking him several times before he finally admitted it.

Your partner is playing a game called "lying by omission." You and your partner had probably talked about your past relationships before, and you remember him mentioning that he was with someone for eight years and that they were engaged. But what your partner is telling you is that since you didn't ask him direct questions like "Were you married?" or "Are you divorced?" he didn't feel obliged or that it was important to share with you that piece of information in your relationship. Basically, he lied to you because you didn't ask him the right questions!

Lying by omission is the most pervasive, insidious and the most common lie used by people globally. It allows liars to manipulate a situation to their advantage by failing to reveal the truth because they were not asked a question directly that pertains to the "truth." This tactic is used to generate false impression as well as to promote something to appear like something that is really not.

3. Denial

Denial, an unwillingness to admit wrongdoing, has long been conceptualized as a mechanism for ego defense. What this means is that it is generally assumed that a person unconsciously denies the reality of a situation because it is simply too painful to bear. However, when disturbed characters or manipulators, in this case, engage in denial, they are not usually in a state of psychological unawareness as a result of a deep inner pain about who they are or what they have been doing. Instead, they more often use denial as a tactic to feign innocence as well as a way to manage the impression of others, especially those who might otherwise have their number.

Some manipulators are so good in this technique that they can successfully manipulate others into second-guessing themselves. Oftentimes, manipulators won't admit when they have done something wrong and will also refuse to look at any role that their behavior patterns may have played in causing problems in their lives. They will not only lie to others but to themselves too about their malicious acts and intentions. If their denial is convincing and forceful enough, others will more likely be successfully manipulated. This is always a tactic to get other people off their backs.

Denial is not only a very effective manipulation tactic, but it's also a definite sign that the person is not about to change their way of behavior. Someone who is unwilling to acknowledge their wrongdoings in the first place is less likely to feel any desire or inclination to correct them. Practicing constant denial by disordered characters and manipulators alike makes them unable to internalize the standards and values of conduct, which in turn makes them less socially responsible.

4. Rationalization

In both logic and psychology, rationalization is a defense mechanism used to justify and/or explain controversial behaviors and feelings in a seemingly logical or rational manner in order to avoid the true explanation. In simpler terms, it means to make excuses. These excuses are usually consciously tolerable, and sometimes even superior and admirable, by reasonable or probable means.

Expert manipulators always have an answer for every hurtful thing they do, and they will always have an excuse in store to justify their behavior no matter what you confront them about. When a person of generally good conscience does something wrong, they will try to find reasons to think that what they did wasn't really that bad in order to assuage that conscience. However, this is not normally the case with manipulators, when they rationalize; their main goal is to try to manage your impression of them. They are trying to convince you that they had no choice but to do what they did, that they meant no harm in the first place or that any reasonable person would have done what they did under the circumstances. This way, they end up misleading you about the nature of both their intentions as well as their character. Just like lying, rationalization is another tactic that manipulators use to resist accepting responsibility, and most of all, as a way to get the better of others.

When a person makes excuses for something, they know is wrong, they are also making a statement about their feelings toward the principle at stake. For example, when a cheating partner keeps making excuses for their behavior, they are making a statement about their feelings toward the wrongness of unfaithfulness. At the same time, they are sending a clear signal that they are likely to repeat the behavior – as long as they continue making excuses for the behavior, repeating it is inevitable. This is because they have not yet submitted themselves to a principle of conduct that is different. This is also why it's important to be aware of people who make excuses for everything because if you accept them not only do you get manipulated, but you also put yourself in a position of having it done to you over and over again.

5. Minimization

Minimization is a lethal type of deception that involves denial coupled with rationalization. When a person uses the tactic of minimization, they are attempting to convince the other person that the wrongful they did wasn't really as harmful or as bad as they know it was and they are also very much aware that the other person thinks it was. This way, they are able to manage the impressions that other people have on them by manipulating them into thinking that no matter the horrible thing they did it does not make them bad.

For instance, minimization language is very common among cheating partners – especially after their affair is exposed. When a cheating partner claims that the affair was a "mistake" or "it was just sex," it is in itself both manipulation and minimization. The partner uses this tactic to maintain control but not to protect their spouse's feelings. Through it, they intend to maintain as much of the illusion as they can and for as long as it's suitable for them.

Additionally, when a person minimizes serious wrongdoings, they are also lying to themselves about the full extent of their behavior problems and character deficiencies. As long as they continue with the act, they will never take the problems they need to correct seriously. Just like any other manipulation tactics, minimization hinders the internalization of standards and values of conduct. It's another way that manipulators use to resist accepting responsibility.

Manipulators are good at disregarding the seriousness of their transgressions, and anyone who accepts their minimizations is for that reason successfully manipulated. Therefore, when he or she uses phrases like "I only did it once" or "You are overthinking things," do not fall for it.

6. Covert intimidation

Intimidation is the intentional behavior done to cause a person to fear harm or injury. Covert intimidation is throwing a person onto the defensive by using subtle, implied, indirect, or veiled threats. This manipulation tactic is much more effective when the manipulator is skilled in communicating determination, resolve, and emotional tenacity, sending the message that the other person is no match for them. This means that the veiled threat is not so much embedded in what is being said or done but rather, the tone or manner employed when the threat is being said or done.

In this tactic, the message is always the same – the manipulator implies that some sort of hell will break out if they get their way or if their dysfunctional behavior is confronted or challenged. Relationships that have partners who use this technique of covert intimidation are often at high risk of being abusive, exploitive, or both.

7. Evasion

In evasion, a manipulator will often try to avoid a subject or sidestep an issue when confronted about their behavior. They use this tactic to keep the attention off their problematic behaviors. They also use it when their true character threatens to be exposed, especially when they are caught off guard without a proper offensive strategy for taking advantage of other people. Therefore, they are quick to dodge any kind of important issue brought to their attention. Instead of giving a straight answer when asked a direct question, they often give rambling, irrelevant, or vague responses as a way of evading or sidestepping the question.

Evasion is a classic tactic that manipulators use to remain in control of situations. Outdated principles of classical psychology used to describe evasion a behavior that manipulators use when they perceive themselves to be under attack and that they are just trying to defend themselves as well as protect their ego. However, this was just a misconception; the real reason manipulators use such tactics is to keep others at a disadvantage in this situation or in the dark. A manipulator will always want to have the advantage over others and not having to play by the same rules as others would like them to. Therefore, tactics like evasion are used to avoid responsibility and also to control and manipulate others.

8. Diversion

Diversion and evasion are often closely associated. Sometimes when you try to pin down someone who is an expert manipulator, they will effectively change the subject and divert the focus on an entirely different issue. This cunning sleight of hand is oftentimes an effective way to keep the focus on almost anything else other than the matter that has been raised. Usually, the focus is even shifted towards the person trying to bring to light the problem behavior, and as a result, they are effectively thrown on the defensive. Also, diversion prompts the other person to lose focus and hinders their pursuit of the truth.

Both diversion and evasion are classical means of deflecting confrontation or concern about problem behaviors. It is self-evident that the manipulator using these tactics has no intention at all of taking responsibility for their behavior or even considering changing it. Rather than be responsible and accountable, all they are trying to achieve is advancing their own agenda and at the same time managing your impression of them.

A perfect example of people who employ these techniques effectively is political talking heads being grilled by news commentators asking them serious questions concerning the policies being endorsed. Most of them stay on the message while remaining convincing and looking good, despite being aware of the flaws in their positions.

Chapter 6 Mind Control

What is Mind Control and How Does it Work?

Mind control is a broad term that can be defined as any technique or method that effectively influences the mind, in one way (or multiple ways) for the purpose of manipulation. Manipulation can produce a variety of outcomes, and used for a variety of reasons, from compliance and obedience to influencing how a person looks at themselves or others to evoke certain responses and behaviors. Essentially, when your actions and behaviors are influenced heavily from an individual or group, you may often dismiss your own doubts or feelings in favor of theirs.

The effects of mind control don't work immediately in most cases, as this would be too obvious and easy to spot.

How does mind control work? Mind control is the desired result of manipulation and related psychological techniques or methods that effectively influence your emotions and mind to bend your will and actions for another person's gain. It can be used to gain power, influence and money or benefits from another person, and maybe applied towards people who are in a position of privilege or in a state of vulnerability, making them a prime target. Once a person establishes a level of trust and confidence over another, they can be "primed" or targeted for mind control. The person seeking this form of dominance may be observant in the other person's habits and behaviors, learning how best to bait them with favorable comments and responses to gain their trust for further manipulation. Mind control and manipulation are almost always used for exploitation purposes. They often begin with seemingly more benign versions of persuasion or coaxing, which later develops into stronger forms of manipulative techniques.

The History of Mind Control and Its Effects Today

When reflecting on the history of mind control, you may think of brainwashing techniques used in prison camps and dangerous cults that have such a detrimental effect on people's minds to the point of permanent harm or death.

Headlines of mass suicide or long-term psychological impairment, Stockholm syndrome, or post-traumatic stress disorder may also come to mind. In everyday life, mind control is just as prevalent as always, though we may not always be aware of it or recognize the signs. The effects of mind control are not always obvious, and often, they influence our decisions, thoughts, and feelings in ways that we are not always aware of. Throughout history, mind control has been used as a means to instill fear and produce obedience among groups of people and can also be used within smaller groups or between individuals to yield powerful control over someone. When this happens, the power dynamic becomes severely imbalanced in favor of the manipulator(s). In countries or regions where people have very little freedom or liberty, certain regimes may have a stronghold over their citizens, by using the threat of imprisonment, punishment and other withholding fundamental rights as a result. Severe impoverishment and lack of proper food and water can often keep people in fear of disobedience or speaking out, for fear they may lose what little they have access to for their families and communities.

Today, mind control is widespread as it has always been. It occurs worldwide within governments, organizations, and between smaller groups and individuals.

In many ways, it's more obvious and present than ever, though we often ignore the signs. Commercial influence and the ability to convince people to buy products they don't need is powerful, especially when people are willing to go into debt or sacrifice their hard-earned income for something less important. Some forms of media and publications may often broadcast or publish certain headlines and events more often than others to provoke a sense of fear or urgency about home invasion or public safety. They may use emotive words and phrases to evoke responses of fear or shock, which causes people to live more cautiously and carefully, without deviating from the "norm."

What are the Signs of Mind Control?

Like manipulation, mind control aims to persuade and influence a person or people's ways of thinking, acting, and behaving to gain a benefit. When people are easily influenced and manipulated, they become more susceptible to practicing or doing things that would normally not consider as an option. The effect or success of mind control can vary depending on the techniques used, the target(s) and the environment. These factors, among others, play an important role in how successful and powerful mind control can be and also provide information on how to spot these signs before they develop further:

1. Isolation

This may seem like a severe case of solitary confinement, though isolation can refer to simply keeping you from friends and family.

This tactic is often used by an abusive partner or spouse to keep their partner away from the comfort and support of friends and family. Isolation can be psychological, in that the manipulator will gradually convince you that one or two family members are trying to control you when they are the one doing the controlling. Over time, if they are successful in persuading you that your family is deceptive or manipulative, they may continue to target friends and co-workers or acquaintances as well, telling you there is something wrong with them, or making you feel as though your friends are insincere, jealous or not truly worthy of your friendship. After a while, friendships and family members fade into the background, and you find yourself more emotionally dependent on the person practicing these mind control techniques. Isolation can effectively keep you from seeking help when you finally realize the dangers of being left alone with someone who does not have your best interest at heart.

Recognizing the early signs of someone or an organization to isolate you from others, even subtly, is vital to avoiding a long-term disaster. Any type of discredit or negativity towards good friends and family should be regarded as a possible sign of control. This tactic will usually occur early in a relationship, where the manipulator realizes a strong bond between you and others.

They see this as a threat to their ability to control you and will do anything in their power to break these relationships to keep you vulnerable to their will. If a group or organization appear inclusive and friendly yet questions the nature of your personal relationships and friendships, it's a sure sign they are seeking to gain more control of your life.

2. Mood Swings and Erratic Behavior

If your partner becomes easily agitated or angry when you disagree with them or makes you feel unworthy of their affection for expressing an honest opinion, they are grooming you to bend to their will. For the manipulator, there is little or no room for any variance in opinion or thought. They will only accept complete submission and agreement.

Anything less will result in erratic mood swings and unpredictable behaviors. In extreme cases, some manipulative people become violent or aggressive. The very threat of this possibility will convince their victims to remain obedient simply out of fear. Recognizing severe changes in mood or emotion, especially when there is no reason or event to trigger the change, is a good reason to avoid someone. Over time, this behavior will escalate and become worse, especially once you discover their tactic and need to escape their manipulate grasp.

3. No Compromises

Mind control, when effective, requires complete and total obedience. There is no room for other thoughts or compromising. In a healthy relationship, all opinions expressed are regarded with respect, even if disagreements or debates are surrounding certain topics. Not allowing another person to express their thoughts without ridicule or judgment can convince them that they are not worthy or compromise. It is also a form of psychological and emotional abuse. This is an easier sign to recognize when even the smallest of decisions or ideas are bent to the will of the manipulator. This can mean anything from choosing a restaurant for dinner or film to watch, which later affects more significant decisions, such as a mortgage or starting a family. Knowing when to spot a lack of compromise can save you a lot of grief later in life, especially where a long-term relationship may form.

Who Uses Mind Control? Organizations, High Control Groups, and People We Know and Encounter in Everyday Life

Who uses mind control, and for what purpose? Many people who are susceptible to the influence of mind control don't often realize they are. There are different people (individuals) and groups that employ mind and thought-control techniques for a variety of reasons.

Understanding their purpose also provides a good explanation for why certain techniques are used and how to recognize them. When we encounter everyday situations, from commuting to work or school, shopping in a grocery store or running errands, we may experience a form of influence or covert manipulation through a sales pitch or billboard ad, without realizing its effect.

If we stopped every time, we noticed an ad, a promotion, a person or representative attempting to "pitch" a sale or ask for a donation, we would then realize how bombarded our mind is with persuasion. In reality, only certain ads or people will catch our attention, while others will slip away.

Chapter 7 Effective Communication and how to Enhance Your Social Skills

Importance of Communication Skills

They are the most important skills that can help you develop and keep friendships and build crucial social networks. Communication skills can also help you take care of your needs, while at the same time being appreciative of the needs of other people. It is common knowledge that no one is born with good communication skills; but like all other skills, you can learn them through trial and error by practicing daily.

Areas of communication that you have to practice regularly include:

- Conversation skills

- Assertiveness

- Non-verbal communication

Point to Note

There are many aspects to effective communication and you may want more help in specified areas such as providing feedback, dealing with conflicts, and learning how to present.

Non-Verbal Communication

A large part of what people communicate to each other nonverbally. What you say to people with your body language or eyes is as important as what you utter. However, your tone of voice and body language does communicate messages to other people regarding your:

- Honesty (do you have any secret intention?)

- Attitude towards the listener (for example contempt and submissiveness)

- Knowledge of the subject

- Emotional state or condition (for example fear and impatience)

Therefore, if you are used to standing far away from other people, deliberately avoiding eye contact, and speaking quietly, you are simply saying, "Please stay away from me!" or "Please do not speak to me!" Sometimes the chances may be that this is not the message that you wish to pass across.

Conversation Skills

One of the most challenging things to do if you have social anxiety is initiating a conversation and keeping it going. It is normal to struggle a bit when you are trying to start a talk because it is not easy to think of the things to say. This is usually the case especially when you are anxious. Besides, some anxious people speak too much, which may sometimes have a negative impression on other people.

Assertiveness

Assertive communication is the expression of your feelings, wants, and needs in an honest way while making sure that you respect those of other people. When you express your thoughts assertively, you prove that you are non-judgmental and non-threatening, and you are responsible for your actions.

The social skills concern the skills required to manage and impact the emotions of other people effectively. Even though this sounds like manipulation, it is essentially initiating a positive emotion and getting others to manifest their emotions positively. In this way, emotional skills can be regarded as the ultimate piece of emotional jigsaw. A revisit of emotional intelligence indicates that it begins with understanding your emotions which is self-awareness competence. Once you have understood your emotions, the next step is to handle them in what is known as the self-regulation. With managed emotions, you can use them to accomplish your goals in what is known as self-motivation. If you understand and handle yourself then you will begin to comprehend the feelings of others in what is regarded as empathy and eventually you will influence them in what is regarded as social skills.

In this manner, social skills will include the ability to persuade and impact skills in others. Social skills will also include communication skills and conflict management skills. If you possess social skills with respect to emotional intelligence then you will also possess leadership skills. Change management skills are part of social skills and building rapport is another social skill applied in emotional intelligence. One must also possess collaboration and cooperation competencies to become socially skilled within the context of emotional intelligence. Against this backdrop, the following is a detailed discussion of requisite competencies to build your social skills within the context of emotional intelligence.

Persuasion and influencing skills

The art of enticing others and convincing them to absorb your ideas is known as persuasion. Persons that are persuasive or have an impact will read the emotional currents in a situation and perfect what they are saying to appeal to spur involved. Persuasion is a function of communication and personality and this demands that you become an effective communicator who is empathetic to others. Winning over people involves trying to convince them to join your course. You must learn to sell your views as a salesperson would do.

Communication skills

Good emotional intelligence requires good communication skills. Learn to listen to others and channel your thoughts and your feelings. Make the people around you understand what is you are communicating and look for the full and open sharing of information. Part of communication ski; s will require that you become prepared to learn about challenges and not just wanting to receive good news. If you are a good communicator you will handle challenging issues directly as opposed to letting problems compile. Ensure that the message that you are packaging is appropriate and then register and act on emotional cues when communicating.

Conflict management skills

Conflicts are unavoidable and sometimes not predictable. Both at home and at work, the art of handling and resolving conflict is important. Conflict management skills begin with becoming aware of the critical tact and diplomacy and how these competencies can be applied to defuse emotive situations. If you are a good conflict manager, you will manage to expose disagreements and help resolve them. Most important is that conflict resolution does not involve you dictating the solution rather helping the affected parties identify the different opinions, the fears and shared understanding to craft a solution. The competence of conflict resolution entails deploying sharing of emotions to motivate debate and open discussion as well as lessening the underlying problems. When resolving conflict emphasize more on the logical position as this is often the shared understanding among the conflicting parties.

Leadership skills

Emotional intelligence and leadership skills are connected in multiple ways. The ability to influence requires that you tune your emotions and those of others to win them over. Influence is a critical attribute of good leadership. It is sometimes called charisma but though leadership skills involving influence goes beyond charisma to match good emotional intelligence. The competencies of good leadership require you to articulate a vision and those other people with it. You do not have to be in a formal leadership position to give leadership. While holding your colleagues accountable, support and direct their performance. Learn to lead by example.

Change management skills

Change catalysts can be effective managers and individuals that make a change to materialize while involving everyone. For all people involved, change tends to create pressure partly because of the fear of unknown. Good change management skills require you to make it an interesting opportunity rather than a threat. Change catalysts acknowledge the importance of change and eliminate barriers. Change catalysts disrupt the status quo and advocate for change. Leading by example is a common attribute of change catalysts to trigger desired adjustments.

Building rapport

It is important to create and maintain constructive relationships with other persons. Mastering this skill will lead to improved relationships and increased the ability to work and succeed in life. Persons that are good with building bonds are great networkers, create and sustain a robust network of connections and contacts. Creating a rapport involves establishing relationships to maintain it healthy. If you exhibit good rapport as a competence then you are likely to have many friends. The essence of building bonds is to value others and being interested in their lives as well as being eager to learn more about them.

Team-working

Persons with good collaboration skills will build good and useful productive working as well as other relationships and there are people who function well with others. All these attributes are vital when building social skills in emotional intelligence. People with collaborative skills will see relationships as critical as the pending task and will value people as much as they consider the activity at hand. If you have collaboration skill then you will actively cooperate, share ideas and plans, and work with others to create an improved whole. The best environment will attract other people to contribute. If you possess the collaboration and cooperative competence then you will actively look out for opportunities for cooperative working. A team will perform better when good team-workers are present in the group and this tends to attract other members to join the team. Good team-workers help the team build an identity and foster commitment.

Chapter 8 Tone and Pitch – Where Verbal meets Non-verbal

You can glean a lot of information from tone of voice. When words are delivered in a certain tone and with a certain emphasis, they can take on different meanings. For example, someone is inviting you to an event, but you sense that the invitation is offered grudgingly. Why do you have that sensation? It's the tone. Does it seem half-hearted? A resigned, or flat tone can indicate that the invitation is being recited in order to either please someone else, or out of social obligation.

Tone, pitch and even the cadence (rhythm) and speed of speaking can make the difference between being heard and being talked over. You can also learn a lot about people's level of confidence from the rate of speed at which they speak. The usual conversational pace is about 140 words per minute. Faster than that and you're perceived to be prattling. Slower than that and you'll either have people hanging on your every word (the current American President comes to mind), or bored to death.

In the popular television show, Seinfeld, when the character, Neuman (who is not well-loved by other characters on the show) appears, the refrain is "Hello, Neuman". But the tone of voice this is delivered in is uniformly venomous. Less a greeting, than a threat! Tone can convey subtext by transforming words in rather surprising ways.

For women readers, this is especially important. Tone and pitch must be carefully modulated, particularly in business circles. Lowering the pitch of your voice causes your words to change in terms of value to the listener, particularly when you're talking to men. Men are known to "zone out" at times, when women speak. It's therefore incredibly important that women modulate their voices, speaking in a manner which commands the attention of others, when you desire to so command it. For women, this is a form of linguistic mirroring. Because the tone of male voices tends to be lower than that of most women, buy mirroring that tonal quality, a sleight of hand is performed in which women may mirror their male fellows and demand that they listen.

The human voice is like an instrument. Vary the tonal quality of what you're saying, adding emphasis at the end of a sentence to add a question mark (which most of us do naturally), or lowering it to impart authority to your words. Pause, if you need to. Consider what will come next. If you've taken the time to compose a thought and believe that it's worth listening to, have the confidence not to blurt. Take as much time delivering the thought in words as you've spent composing it.

A fascinating aspect of the quality of people's voices is that they can tell us a lot about the people speaking. Everyone has a vocal quality that is habitual, to some extent. Often, we're unaware of it. Some people sound whiny and nasal, without even knowing it. Others sound warm and effusive, by nature. Then, some folks have a flat, monotonous quality to their voices. Sometimes, culture and language can affect tone and pitch. Usually, though, tone and pitch imply an attitude that is unspoken, but evident. Paying attention to the quality of people's voices and the sensation experienced when you hear them will train your ears to factor voice into your evaluation of those around you.

Remember, they may be doing the same with you. It's important that you're aware of how you sound. You may want to practice reading out loud to get a sense of how you sound to others. You can video or record yourself and play it back. How do you sound to yourself? What mannerisms are you displaying for others to read? What is your face saying? Getting a read on yourself is a good foundation for applying your self-knowledge to your interpretation of those around you. When you're able to take an objective look at the signals you're sending, you'll be better able to read them in others.

Dress and aesthetics

If you invited someone to your wedding and they showed up in flip flops, sweatpants and a baseball cap, as if they had just been shopping in their local grocery store, or had rolled out of bed and not even showered, what would be your conclusion? You would probably conclude that this person did not care about your wedding and was, very likely, not happy to be there. What another conclusion could be drawn?

A persons sartorial and personal care habits are visible signs of their attitudes toward themselves and others. Particularly in the workplace, a lackadaisical approach to one's appearance can indicate a lack of concern for the quality of the work, the standards of the workplace, or both. People who present themselves well look confident, because they feel confident. Their hair is groomed. Their clothing is attractive, clean and presentable and their nails are clean. They know they look good. Those who tend not to care very much about the details of presentation tend not to be perceived as competent and perhaps as suffering from low self-esteem.

So it's extremely important that you send the right message to others by presenting yourself as one who deems appearance to be of some importance. That is not to say that everyone's expected to be a preening peacock, as that style of presentation can be just as distracting (if not, more so) than neglect. Whether we choose to admit it or not, people tend to judge others on their appearance and if yours isn't well-curated, or curated at all, with no concession to public standards, you will not be well-regarded.

As I've said above, a lack of concern for personal appearance can indicate a number of realities under the surface, but sometimes, looks are deceiving. People who tend not to care a great deal about their appearance can be intensely intellectual and engaged in their work. This is particularly true of computer programmers, academics and others involved in work that involves a high level of focus. There's more to some people than meets the eye, so it's always wise to factor in variables when reaching an evaluation. As you'll know if you've read this far, knowing about people is about a lot of little things – not just one big thing.

As for you, this section will have made clear the kind of message that's genuinely appealing – pride in one's appearance. That's expressed by an overall attention to grooming and appropriateness of dress. A sense of style is a bonus. If you don't have one, spend some time thinking about how those you admire present themselves and ask yourself how you might create that effect yourself. If you lack a lot of savvy in that department, remember to keep it simple, streamlined and tidy. This will send the message that you care, are confident about yourself, but also professional. That's probably the most important factor, especially for those of you reading who hope to learn the skills involved in developing influential gifts. First impressions are lasting impressions. You can be the smartest man or woman in the room, but if you look like an unmade bed, it won't matter one bit.

All the factors listed are elements of communication. Everything you say, do and wear, every expression on your face, every gesture and every high and low in the tone and pitch of your voice tells a tale about what you intend. Knowing how to honestly evaluate yourself in all these departments is a solid way of developing your influential heft. When you know yourself and your habits and can objectively see them as elements of your own communicative style, knowing you can improve some or all of them, you'll be better equipped to influence others. By deconstructing your own style, you'll have a window into how others are communicating with you, using all these elements.

Lance Burdett, a communications professional who has worked as National Advisor to the New Zealand Police Crisis Negotiation Teams, says that the importance of effective communication can't be overstated. He is well known for his insistence that effective communication can diffuse anger and correct abusive behavior. He says that good communication skills (including evaluation of the communication styles of others), are the basis for an ability to defuse potentially dangerous situations, and to help reduce the toxicity of potentially explosive environments. It is, for example, very tempting to react with anger when someone speaks to you angrily. But does that get you where you want to be in terms of advancing your agenda? Nothing could be further from the truth. Having the ability to measure your response, especially in tense situations, can be crucial to a satisfactory outcome. Finesse and attention to detail are key in situations in which anger can turn to violence in a heartbeat. How effective these skills are in your everyday life is highlighted by their importance in police work, when their successful application can mean life or death.

By understanding social psychology and having the requisite inter-personal skills, you have the ability to meet people where they stand and to appeal to what matters to them. Having the skill of being able to effectively read and interpret the communicative clues people send us, both verbally and non-verbally, is the basis for social and professional success.

Following is a brief summary of making your spoken communication more effective and clearer:

Be specific

Say what you mean. Mean what you say. Ensure that the message others receive is the one you intend and that your gestures, expressions, body language and tone match. There should be no perceived dissonance between these various elements of your communicative style, but when you speak with conviction and honesty, that won't be a problem. Before you can convince others, or influence them, you have to buy what you're selling, yourself. You're your first best or worst customer. Be sure of your message and be sure it's clear, concise and keyed to the person or people you're talking to, in order to find the common ground, you seek.

Read the signs

Good communication is a matter of persuasion, not force. Do not, for example, try to convince yourself that the listener is fully engaged with the conversation in order to flatter yourself. Sometimes people are just being polite and trying not to offend you. They may be bored, offended, or tired. Pay attention to the expressions and body language of those you're talking to. Don't be a bore. It is imperative that you work on understanding the art of non-verbal communication so that you can take an accurate reading of whatever situation you are in. Proficiency in understanding people's behavior in social interactions is key to navigating them successfully. Knowing who you're talking to is of vital importance. While you may have grand ideas about the value of what you're saying, watch the listener to ensure you're not deluding yourself.

Chapter 9 How to Improve Your Positivity

Positive reasoning has been comprehended and utilized in different ways, sometimes to the extent of an entirely inappropriate meaning. Individuals misuse the influence of this incredible practice and recommend that it will draw in cash or wealth: "Be positive, and you will have anything you need!"

No, you will not! And it is not the reason for practicing your mind to think along these lines. This is actually one of the principal reactions to the book, "The Secret." Just by doing great, you can have anything you desire. That is a lie, period!

The advantages of reasoning and feeling positive are, in reality, beneficial. They will trigger other positive marvels throughout your life. You will put both your soul and body in an exceptional state with the capacity of achieving great things. Joy and euphoria will emanate from you wherever you go. Life will appear to be greatly improved. Your frame of mind will improve, as well as the world's disposition toward you.

The reward for thinking positively is a delightful life full of energy and motivation. Likewise, it will unquestionably help you in your financial undertakings. These are some of the incredible practices that will put you destined for success in your everyday life:

- Help others in need.

You know, it is not about you. Help other individuals and really care. Try not to do it only for the sake of doing it, however. Demonstrate some sympathy and empathy. Have a go at placing yourself in their shoe, and view the world through their perspective. At that point, do your best to support them. You have no clue what this can accomplish for you.

- Get used to walking outdoors.

The impact of this single walking outdoors can be incredible. Indeed, even research demonstrates that this activity can support your state of mind, all things considered. Get it done and see the outcomes.

- Laughter is the best medicine.

Our body is the instrument of our mind, yet it is additionally obvious that our contemplations and demeanor are particularly identified with our body due to the manner in which we work. We will, in general, think according to what we see, hear, taste, smell, and feel. So, if you smile, you can quickly feel it, and your mind will react to this. You will begin feeling better and with positivity. It will not just lift up your state of mind; it will influence every other person who interacts with you to feel the same way. You can choose to smile only for the sake of it, or you can think about a circumstance, an occasion, an individual, or anything that puts you in a state of joy. Both of them will work great. You can simply head toward your mirror, take a gander at yourself and will yourself to smile. This works incredibly well. Very soon, it will end up infectious. Have in mind that giggling and grinning can also fix maladies and wretchedness! That is, as of now, deductively demonstrated. Smile regularly, and your energy will continue to expand more every time you do it.

- Volunteer and contribute more to your community. Think about the different ways in which you can improve your community. Maybe you can help with cleaning the parks in your neighborhood? Shouldn't something be said about helping people in the neighborhood library? This one will be peculiar yet surely intriguing. What about visiting detainees and helping in reaching out? Keep in mind that the more you give in your everyday life, the more you receive something in return. Life will consistently remunerate you ten times for each good thing that you do. Choose how you can give back to the community, and after that, do what needs to be done. Inspiration will turn into your characteristic mindset that appears to make your organization consistent.

- Participate in yoga and meditation. These two exercises will never neglect to support your inspiration. They will assist you in gaining control over your considerations, and your mindfulness will be increased. You will end up being mindful at the present minute and what is happening in your mind. Positive considerations will end up normal as you practice these abilities.

- Exercise more.

Truly, this is a significant undertaking for your health and mind. Pick any physical activity that you like and practice it routinely. You can run, climb mountains, or take swimming lessons, or you can take classes in hand-to-hand fighting. You will be enthusiastic about life, energetic, and motivated. Your state of mind will change as well. It is highly unlikely that physical activity will not make you feel positive. Do what needs to be done for your mind and body.

- Offer thanks every day.

Write an appreciation diary, or essentially compose on a sheet of paper five things that you are thankful for. Read this list multiple times every day, starting at the beginning of the day and then around early afternoon and before sleeping. The more things you can incorporate into the rundown, the better. These things should make you feel better and positive about yourself and life when all is said and done. Appreciation is the key to a tranquil, cheerful, and positive way of life.

- Sing a little more.

When life hits you hard, or you make a mistake, sing your problems away. Pick a tune that truly makes you feel happy, and begin playing it in your mind until stress leaves you. The melody can be one which makes you feel glad. It very well may be one that incites giggling and delight in your heart. Is there any tune that you can consider your happy song? This may be something that instantly puts a smile all over face each and every time you hear it. Great music has consistently been an incredible instrument for changing one's temperament. It will never fail to make you feel positive, so consider singing whenever you can, especially at trying times.

- Remember that everything that happens to you is on you.

You can't blame others for the outcomes you get in your life. Every one of our outcomes come as an immediate consequence of our activities and behavior in our everyday life. Our activities and behavior are the immediate consequences of our considerations, decisions, and sentiments. Only you have the ability to control your frame of mind involved your considerations and emotions. You pick the things that you give your regard to, so instead of whimpering and whining, quit accusing the conditions, the government, the economy, and God. It is your fault that you have given these things a chance to happen. Assume full liability to your actions, and your life will turn out to be considerably more positive!

- Make a compliment to other people regularly.

If putting blame on others makes a person feel awful, the opposite of it, which is giving compliments, can make you feel better. The person receiving your compliment will feel better, but you will also feel good. When was the last time you gave a true compliment to somebody, and this compliment came straight from the heart? In the event that you can't recollect it, the time has come to consider doing this whenever you see someone you know. Keep in mind that in case you're searching for the great sides in others, this is an impression of the great sides in you. What's more, be sincere and real when you compliment individuals!

- Breathe in and out regularly.

Have you realized that our awareness is exceptionally associated with our method for relaxing? In particular, yogis and priests have found, in the past, that our considerations are legitimately associated with the manner in which we relax. When we begin breathing gradually and somewhere down in our tummy, by using 100% of our lung's limit, our contemplations appear to back off, and we become progressively loose. Life essentially backs off; all types of pressure leaves both the mind and body and the person who inhales this way picks up lucidity and mindfulness. This training will not just quiet you down; it will influence your well-being and regulate your blood flow better. It will support the movement of your cerebrum, and it will never neglect to improve your state of mind. Breathing is the embodiment of life, so begin mindful breathing as a daily exercise. Essentially, begin practicing this until it turns into a consistent propensity. Inhale somewhere down in your stomach, and fill it like an inflatable. Rather than breathing in shallow breaths in the chest, extend your midsection as much as you can.

The more you practice this system, the more profound and progressively viable your breaths will become. Your cognizance will be clearer, and lucidity and internal harmony will take place. This will never neglect to support your general inspiration.

- Be in a positive environment.

What are your companions like? Does your manager at work have a positive temperament? Is it accurate to say that they are fun and diverting or not so much? Great organizations consistently make a difference! If you happen to associate with negative and burdensome individuals, you can stand to change your way of life in the same way. It is important that your environment is positive since it will be the source of your vitality. It will influence you each and every time.

More often than not, we are affected by a huge amount of cynicism in our lives. We are always besieged with weight and upsetting circumstances, yet it is our decision on how we will react to them. We can assume liability and choose to be in full control over our frame of mind, or we can live step-by-step, letting the influx of life take us wherever it goes.

Carry on with your life in the manner that you want to live it! Quit being a casualty of outside conditions, and choose to pick a positive point of view. Also, make a recollection. It is the little things that have a significant effect on our lives. So, take a full breath at the present time, and state how thankful you are for everything in your life.

Chapter 10 The Most Powerful Mind-Power Tool

Humans spend countless hours seeking new ways to work just about anything. Through endless hours of research, they pour over books and journals looking for the message that will tell them the secret to harnessing mind power. Many never realize that the most powerful mind power tool is already on board and just aching to be used. It is the human brain, the mind itself.

Every time a person practices a new habit or thinks a new thought, they make a new pathway in the brain. Every time the habit is used, or the idea is thought, the nerve pathway becomes even stronger. The human brain is wired at birth to be an efficient machine and it is ready, from birth, to make an ever-increasing amount of nerve pathways and to strengthen the pathways that are used the most.

Sometimes thoughts and habits need to be changed for the improvement of the person. When people decide that they would like to make a change in their lives, there will be a period of adjustment. This is true whether the change is mental, emotional, or physical. During this period of adjustment, there will be some level of discomfort. When a habit or a thought is already formed, it has made its own path in the brain. When a stimulus is seen or heard, the message travels along the preset nerve pathway to the spot in the brain that controls that thought or habit. In order to change a thought or a habit, it is necessary for the nerve path to be changed. Until the nerve path is changed, the old nerve path will remain in the brain. The discomfort comes from the brain trying to automatically access the old pathway and the new pathway at the same time. This is painful for the brain to do.

It is easy to become frustrated when the brain goes back to its old patterns of thought and habit. Never fall into the habit of placing blame on a lack of willpower. Willpower has nothing to do with it. It is a very difficult thing to override preset pathways in the brain. The brain is a very powerful tool. When will power fails and mistakes happen, remember to use kindness and compassion in dealing with the failure. The brain is very efficient at doing what it does. The only way to change the pathways in the brain is to keep working on new pathways that will eventually obliterate the old, undesirable ones.

The brain needs a clear understanding that changes are about to take place and new pathways are about to be laid down. Remind the brain that new habits and new thoughts will be replacing the old ones. Blaming failure on a lack of will power is a self-defeating statement. The process of making new nerve paths in the brain takes hard work and time. It will help to keep reminding oneself of the impending change. By doing this over and over, it makes the process no longer about possible character flaws. The focus is now put on the habit of thought that is being built.

Is it possible to build new nerve pathways in the brain? Yes, it is possible, and it can be done. If more proof is needed, just compare the adult brain to the baby's brain. Every current habit and thought a person have is the direct result of having spent time practicing them over and over until they created a pathway in the brain. New pathways can be created. Think of it this way: they already have. The baby's brain has no idea of anything. It has no thoughts or habits. Every nerve path currently in the brain was practiced until it became a part of the brain. Think of the baby. The baby lies around day after day and does baby things. Then one day the baby notices the shiny rattle that mommy is waving in front of its little face. The baby wants the rattle. As the baby is waving its tiny arms around, the mommy puts the rattle close enough so the baby can touch it with its wavering hand. After a few of these sessions, the baby gets the idea that if the arm is in the air it can touch the rattle. A nerve pathway is beginning to grow. So, the baby decides to lift its arm to actively reach for the rattle. The baby will be unsuccessful at first because the arms will wave wildly and will not connect with the rattle. One day, the baby will actually grab the rattle, and the nerve pathway is then complete.

While this may seem like a very simple example, it is exactly how nerve pathways are created in the brain. Every action, thought, or habit has its own nerve pathway. All pathways must be created. No one was born knowing to sit in front of the television and mindlessly eat dip with chips. No one was born lamenting the excess pounds they carry in strange places. No one was born hating their body. All behaviors are learned, good and bad. And the bad ones can be replaced with good ones.

So, if the ability to program negative thoughts into the brain exists, then the ability to disrupt those negative thoughts with positive thoughts also exists. The brain can be reprogrammed. It is a powerful tool, and its main function is to turn thoughts into reality. The brain is always working, so why not use the power of the brain to benefit rather than harm? Just because a particular habit or thought has been around all forever does not mean it needs to stay. Use the power of the brain to choose new habits and thoughts to focus on and replace the old, negative thought pathways in the brain.

The new thought needs to be believable; the new habit needs to be doable. It does not really good to try to stick to a habit that is impossible to accomplish or to try to believe a thought that is unbelievable. After years of seeing the reality of an obese body, it would be nearly impossible to suddenly believe that the image in the mirror is that of a skinny person. But the brain will likely accept something that mentions learning to take care of the body or learning to accept the body in order to correct its flaws. The brain will turn a belief in reality. Believing a positive thought will lead to quite a different result than the ending where only negative thoughts are present.

Be prepared to repeat and repeat some more. The primary key to being able to make a new habit stay is repeating it constantly. The more a new, desirable habit is practiced, the more the brain begins to accept it. The nerve path becomes stronger every day. With constant practice, this new nerve path will become the path the brain will prefer to use, and the old one will cease to exist.

In any case, be sure to allow enough time to effectively create a change. Accept the starting point and constantly visualize the ending point. Accept the fact that the path to the goal of a new habit or thought will not be easy or perfect. The path will almost never travel in a straight line. Sometimes people fall completely off the path, and that is okay too. Just get back up and get back on. Do not get sidetracked by the idea that this journey will be easy and carefree because it will not be. Just keep thinking of the new nerve pathway that will be created by the new thought or habit and it will eventually become a reality.

Most of the pathways in the brain are stored in the subconscious mind. This is the part of the mind that is always working without always being thought of. Think of learned skills like tying shoes, zipping a coat, and pouring milk into a glass. These were all learned behavior whose nerve pathways are firmly set in the subconscious part of the mind. This part of the brain is the bank of data for all life functions.

The communication between the conscious mind and the unconscious mind works in both directions. Whenever a person has a memory, and emotion, or an idea, it is rooted in the subconscious mind and translated to the conscious mind through mind power. The subconscious has the power to control just about anything a human does regularly.

For example, during meditation steady, deep breathing is usually practiced. The control of the breath is brought from the subconscious mind and given to the conscious mind to tell it to control the breathing. Once a pattern of deep steady breathing is begun by the conscious mind, the subconscious mind takes over and keeps the set rhythm going until it is told to stop. This is done by a conscious end to the deep breathing or an encounter with an outside stimulus like stress. The subconscious mind also processes the great wealth of information received daily and only passes along to the conscious mind those things that are necessary for the brain to remember.

When sending thoughts from the conscious mind to the subconscious mind, the brain will only send those thoughts that are attached to great emotion. The only thoughts that remain in the subconscious are those that are kept there with strong emotions. Unfortunately, the brain does not know the difference between positive emotions and negative emotions. Any strong emotion will work. Both negative emotions and positive emotions can be quite strong. Also, unfortunately, negative emotions tend to be stronger than positive emotions.

Step one in learning to use the power of the subconscious part of the mind will be to eliminate any thoughts that come with negative emotions. Also, negative mental comments will also need to cease. Fears will usually come true, specifically because they are drowning in negative emotion. This is why negative ideas need to be eliminated because they can be very harmful roadblocks on the road to harnessing brain power.

One best practice to use to get rid of negative thoughts is to counter them with positive thoughts. This will take time and practice, but it is a very powerful and useful technique. Whenever a negative thought pops in the conscious mind, immediately counter it with a positive thought that is dripping with strong emotion. The actual truth will come out somewhere in between the two thoughts.

Another way to counter negative emotions is to delete them, just like using a remote control. When a negative thought comes into the conscious mind, imagine destroying it. Imagine writing that thought on paper and burning it. Imagine pointing a remote control at the thought and pressing a huge delete button. Whatever form used to imagine deleting the thought, the important thing is to get rid of it before it can take hold in the subconscious mind.

Find something energizing and use it to reach a goal. Those things that are found to be energizing bring boundless energy to positive thoughts. It is often necessary to invent motivation, at least in the beginning, to learn to create new habits and thoughts. But with a bit of practice and a lot of positive thought, new positive habits will soon be burned into the subconscious mind and the old negative thoughts and habit will fade away.

More Effective Techniques To Influence Others

Along with all the techniques that you have learnt so far, here are a few more, which if you work on committedly will help you achieve the desired results and always achieve success when it comes to manipulating others.

Generate Urgency

To influence, you need to create urgency. Unless you do that, oftentimes, people will not respond as positively as you hope them to. Creating urgency means that you create a scenario or paint a picture of the problem at hand in a manner that it appears as a pressing issue making the other person feel he/she must act as you want. If you want your friend to file for medical insurance, make her feel how urgent that is and how she must not wait another minute to act on it.

Here are some tactics you can use to create urgency in order to manipulate others.

Ask Probing Questions: Asking the right and often probing questions is just the trick that can help you create earnestness in someone to act as desired. If you are tired of your partner not taking his debt issues seriously, ask questions such as 'What problems are we suffering because of financial issues?', 'What are your concerns about your ever-increasing debt?' and 'Is your debt the reason your self-esteem is dwindling?' Make sure to ask the questions with concern in your tone and facial expressions so the other person feels your apprehension and then becomes stimulated to take the desired action.

Give Examples: Another effective tactic to create urgency is to illustrate examples of other people who went through similar experiences, and ended up suffering in the end because they failed to take the right action at the right time. If you wish for your best friend going through depression to get therapy instead of staying engulfed in the darkness all alone, talk to him about how another friend went through the same traumatic episode, but recovered soon after because she had a therapist by her side. Reinforce the urgency by talking about the problem and sharing relevant examples.

Make them Visualize: Visualization is an incredibly effective technique that does not only help you become more invested in your work and put in extra effort to achieve your goals, but also helps you in influencing others as well.

When you wish for someone to oblige to your commands, paint them a beautiful picture of how doing that chore will benefit them. Make them visualize the end outcome and have all their senses involved in the experience so they become fully immersed in the visualization and are then motivated to take the required action.

If you want your students to do well in a certain internship they have signed up for, help them visualize how doing it well will benefit them in the long run and help them land a great job. Make them visualize the sights, sounds, expressions, feelings, sensations and even tastes associated with success. For instance, you can ask them to think of their most favorite ice cream and think of having that when they are successful. Similarly, you can make them think of the sound the ATM makes when your money is about to come out and how you would hear those sounds and feel the touch of crisp dollar bills when you land a fantastic, well paid job.

When you make someone completely involved in an imagination, it targets and influences their subconscious and imbeds relevant suggestions in it. When your subconscious mind becomes focused on a certain outcome, it then makes you work towards achieving that outcome.

Pinpoint the Scarcity: Earnestness can easily be created by using the principle of scarcity. If you want someone to oblige to your demands, let them know how a certain thing is scarce or an offer is only available for a limited time. For instance, if you wish your friend to apply for a scholarship grant for her M.Phil. thesis as soon as possible, let her know how the offer ends in 2 days and how she will miss out on a wonderful opportunity by missing it out. If you want your friends to go out on a food festival with you, inform them of how it ends tonight and how all of you will miss a lifetime experience if you do not go today.

While creating urgency, try not to force the other person into doing something. People who are smart enough to realize this tactic are likely to feel offended by it and then distance themselves from you for a while. Thus, do employ the tactics, but very cautiously so people do not feel upset by anything.

Be Aware of Your BATNA

BATNA refers to your 'best alternative to a negotiated agreement' and is your preferred fallback option that you resort to when things do not go, as you want. It is different from the bottom line, which refers to a fixed position that limits the options available to you and keeps you from discovering new actions.

Knowing your BATNA means that you think through a certain situation to come up with different scenarios wherein things do not happen as desired and then opt for a settlement that appeals to you the most. You need to assess the different alternatives available to you and then opt for the most promising substitute that suits you the most.

If, however, you begin negotiation with a bottom line in your demand, you are likely not to explore any other promising options and may have to settle only for it if the negotiations do not go through as planned. Let us share with you an example to explain this better.

If you are trying to get your charity program funded by some big MNC's and are in talks with a few potential sponsors, you need to begin with asking for complete 100% sponsorship that includes every aspect of the event. Your plan B can be to cut it down by 10% or by eliminating one activity from the package instead of asking for only 50% funds as soon as the sponsors reject your initial proposal. If you present different alternatives, it is likely you can get 70% funds and some added benefits instead of just settling for a small amount of funds.

Similarly, if you wish for a colleague to help you out with a project, give him different options instead of withdrawing your request or asking him to do just a little bit if the first initial request of help is unacceptable to him.

Always be aware of your BATNA and present it in an interesting way while offering benefits of doing that to the concerned individual.

Make Use of Objective Criteria

When trying to persuade someone to carry out a certain task, make use of objective criteria. Settle on a framework based on objective criteria using facts, figures, statements and underlying interests, needs, goals and opinions.

For instance, while having an interdepartmental discussion in the company regarding the launch event of a new service, you become quite convinced that you need to rush it to the market as soon as you can. Now if you wish for the entire team to understand that, you need to provide evidence in form of marketing data and tie it in with how all the team members will benefit from incentives and promotions if the launch goes as planned and receives an overwhelmingly positive response as desired.

When choosing objective criteria for a certain matter, take into consideration factors such as market value, legal standards, contractual terms, mission and objectives, vision and other factors according to the nature of the problem.

Be the Authority on the Matter

People like listening and following someone they perceive as an authority figure. If you wish for others to listen to you attentively and dance to your tune, you need to come off as an authority figure on a certain subject matter. If you want someone to take action against physical abuse and end the vicious cycle of codependency she/he is involved in, tells her/him how you have been through the same or dealt with people who underwent that trauma and how putting an end to that pain is crucial for their betterment right now.

To be an authority, you need to have command over the topic and be fully aware of the ins and outs related with it so you have complete knowledge on the issue and can convince others about it easily. If you want your business partner to buy certain software for your small business, become convinced about it first and use your knowledge about it to persuade him then.

Carry out an in-depth research on the issue to collect as much data on it as possible and then study it on your own to brush your knowledge of it. It is only when you are well versed on it that you can share it with others, educate others about it and influence them in the desired manner.

Bring in the Element of Empathy

Empathy never goes to waste and always does the trick of winning people over. When being empathetic towards people, remember not to do it just to fulfill your ulterior motives. Empathy is about feeling the pain of others as your own and is something so beautiful that it needs to be incorporated positively in all your actions.

Be your compassionate, loving self with others and be as empathetic as you can with people you genuinely care about. Feel the pain of others, be around them to show your support and do not push anyone to do something he/she feels uncomfortable about. You will build a fantastic rapport with people once you become empathetic towards them and this will only make it easier for you to inspire them.

Remember the Names and Faces of People

An effective way to shower attention on someone especially someone you have only met once or twice is to remember their face and name. People love to build connection with others and when they do, they quickly feel drawn towards that very person. When you meet someone, ask his/her name and use it a couple of times during the conversation so you imbed it in your subconscious mind. Also, pick any prominent facial feature and tie it with that person's name so you remember it easily.

The next time you meet him/her, greet him/her using their name affectionately and it will definitely cheer him/her up drawing them towards you.

Try to make written notes of all the practices you try and how each works out in your favor. Certain tactics work well with certain people while some don't. Therefore, write down about how you implement each tactic so you can keep track of your performance and improve on it the next time.

Chapter 11 Persuading Someone with Your Words

First of all, we need to know what Persuasion is. We come up with too many different answers when the question is about persuasion. Some People may think about commercial advertising that they see around them in which someone urges to purchase a certain product over another. Some may think about persuasion in the form of politics where a leader may try to sway the voter's opinion to get another vote.

Both examples are a kind of persuasion because in both cases the message is trying to change the thinking or perception of the other person. It can find many times in our daily life which is a very powerful force as well as the major influence on society. every kind of advertising, mass media, digital/social media, political rallies all are influenced by how persuasion is working and in turn how it is working to persuading the subject as well.

Persuasion itself is a key to mind control among the various others like brainwashing, hypnosis bullying, Manipulation. But, there is little difference between it and other forms of mind control like brainwashing and hypnosis need the subject in isolation in order to change the mind and thinking of subject, Manipulation works on just one person to get the final goal of manipulator while persuasion can work with just person and also with a group of people if we want to use it on larger scale any group can also be convinced through persuasion. It is rather more effective or we can say is dangerous because it can change the perception of the whole group or society rather than just changing the mind of a single person or subject.

Sometimes people make false impressions that they are immune from persuasion. many people think that they are smart enough that they will see any sales pitch that is thrown their way, whether the sales are selling a product or service or some new idea, these people try to find their logic. In some cases, it can be true because of no fall for everything that is told by someone, especially when that is different from your own beliefs than it does not matter how strong argument is done. On the other hand, many people will be able to avoid the advertisement for a fancy car and television or whatever is new in the market. Many times, the act of persuasion can be much subtler what we think of, now it becomes more difficult to subject to form their own opinion about what they are being told.

Now with the other forms of mind control, there are certain elements that need to see in case of persuasion, these elements exactly define persuasion and will help to recognize it in a more comfortable zone. Persuasion can be defined now as a process of communication where someone can change the thought process and point of view of a certain individual without even letting him know about it. This thing makes persuasion different from other forms of mind control means the subject can use his/her own choice for deciding on any matter even if the tactics of persuasion are going to make a change in the mind or perception of that subject in some particular direction.

The elements which define persuasion, even more, better are the following:

- Persuasion is always symbolic it can utilize sound, images; words are logics to get the point across.

Let us have look at this element in more detail that is persuasion need to be symbolic. as if we think about to persuade someone, we need to let that subject know very first about it or we need to act in a certain way that why should that person have to change their thought or perspective toward a particular topic or thing, for this process we need to include some sound or images or facts to get a new point across. Apart from that words are necessary to start a debate or argument so that you can put your point of view to that person. Pictures are even the best evidence to convince someone for anything that is required and can persuade the subject to go one way or other. And lastly, the nonverbal cues can also be possible to use some particular cases of persuasion. But they are not going to be as effective as words and images.

- Self-persuasion is the key part of this process, as the subject will always have the freedom to choose in case of persuasion, usually the subject is not coerced, or the subject is free to choose his/her own decision.

The second one is the thing that it is unique about persuasion that it allows the subject to have some form of free will, the subject can think about any decision as per their own choice. For mostly it is no matter how hard someone is trying to persuade the person, he/she will not go for it. For example, we see thousands of advertisements of cars of various brands. But, if we don't need a new vehicle or not liked the brands, we are not going to convince our self to go out and purchase the new car. Therefore, it allows much more freedom of choice that is available in other forms of mind control.

- It involves the agent deliberately attempting to influence the subject or group of people.

Thirdly, it can be used deliberately to influence the thinking or point of view of others; this is obvious even when you do not try this trick of persuasion with a purpose or we can say you are not trying to influence the subject purposefully, you are not using persuasion to get the change. A persuader will try different tactics to think in the same way as the subject do. it can be sometimes simple enough like a small debate and sometimes it may take more efforts like pieces of evidence, nonverbal signals apart from the words itself.

- The persuasive messages can be transmitted through various ways like face to face, internet, radio or television, or the communication can be verbal or non-verbal.

The Modern Form of Persuasion

Over time, everything has got change. Persuasion has been evolved and changed from its original form or beginning. it has been around for many years even from the ancient time. But, the art and process of persuasion are not that same now as it was earlier or way back then. There have been many changes that have done to the art of persuasion as to how it is used in modern time. There are a few key elements of modern-day persuasion. Let us discuss those keywords further like how it is used and how it can affect society as a whole. Now there are five ways how modern persuasion is different how it was used in the past. These five ways are the following:

- Earlier, persuasion was used in just writing and in debates among the elites. The occurrence of persuasion was not a big thing and it was not quite often to see. But now in modern times, it is difficult to get someplace without persuasion around you. It is now much more a part of modern life than it has been at any other time in history.

- Persuasion travels very fast, back in ancient it could take weeks or more time for the persuasive message to get one point to another. This limits the impact of persuasion because most people will be unaware of that message and most of the acts of persuasion had to be done face to face context. But in modern times communication persuasive message covers large distance through the internet, radio, and television. It has a greater role when it can be spread quickly. Persuasion can mean a lot of money like companies have discovered the power of persuasion as the more effective they are at persuading customers to purchase their product the more money they will make. Companies like public relations, advertising agencies, and marketing firms are thoroughly working under the tactic of persuasion mean their business will be grown up only if there is the existence of persuasion.

- Now as days persuasion becomes subtler than it was in the past. Ancient was the time when a persuader was announcing his/her ideas loudly for the whole group to hear or to subject with the hope that they will change their mind about something. Those days are over now and the process of persuasion has become more discrete than ever while it is possible to find out loud and face to face persuasion in today's world too, we can see that in form of advertising and many others are following a subtler route.

- The process of persuasion has become far more complex now. The subjects who are targeted are more diverse than earlier, sometimes even it is harder to find out. For example. In the past, it was like if somebody wants to purchase something, they need they were going to a specific store and buy the necessary product. But now a days the scenario has been changed like if we want to purchase something that is needed, we find the stores with various departments and sections where it is not that easy to find first the needed item but we there are more than one options are available for everything and it makes the process of persuasion more complex than ever.

Methods of Persuasion

Persuasion methods we can call them often as persuasion strategies persuasion tactics. There is not even single one method by which someone can persuade the others, or convince in a certain way. the agent can switch the subject from the mind of the subject by talking something else and showing some evidence on the other hand or the agent may be able to use some kind of force to let the subject do what agent needs, they can perform some service for the subject or can offer something to subject. Let us see more details for these sections of persuasion.

Chapter 12 Non-Verbal Communication

Knowing where you are and who you're with concern more than geography and facial recognition. Understanding the subtext of human interactions is a means of managing them more effectively. Understand the meaning of a glare thrown at you from across a crowded room by someone who doesn't like it is pretty simple. What's not so simple is your decision about formulating a response, right then and there. In understanding what people are trying to tell you without words, you gain a confidence in your social interactions based on wisdom about people. It takes time to learn. It is, in fact, a life's work, but there's much you can do right now to improve your ability to more accurately gauge what people around you are thinking, feeling and perhaps, hoping will happen, where you're concerned.

Here are some common ways people speak without words:

Hand gestures

In some cultures, hand gestures can easily be read by others. In fact, every culture in the world uses them. In some cultures, though, hand gestures have communicative pride of place. One of these is, of course, Italy. In fact, the people of Italy are rather notorious for their tendency to talk with their hands.

Some of these gestures are found in other cultures, but many are peculiar to Italy. Italian art can be seen to feature some of these, like the *ficha* (meaning "fig"), in which the four fingers are brought together with the thumb. Today, this gesture is used to express a capacity crowd in a public facility (restaurant, sports arena, coffee shop). Alternatively, the same gesture when accompanied by a pointed back and forth motion of the upper arm, bent at the elbow means "what?", or "what in the hell?", even "what's wrong with you?"

But there are many universal hand gestures that can reveal what someone is feeling, as you engage with them. Throwing the hands up in the air is a universal expression of exasperation. Putting a hand in front of the body, with a straight arm is universally understood to mean "stop". But there are other ways the hands can tell us what's going on inside the people we engage with.

Gestures in which the palms are turned downward indicate authority. With the arms outstretched, this type of gesture can also indicate a sense of superiority or domination. However, when the hands are used in gestures with the palms down, in the course of a conversation or business negotiation, the person gesturing is indicating an unwillingness to concede a point. When part of a firm, downward motion (like chopping), the message is "no".

Alternatively, gestures involving open palms indicate an earnest interest in reconciling a point, or a willingness to reach a concession or agreement. Palms facing up are an indication of openness.

Hands clenched in fists (unless you're about to engage in a fistfight), normally indicate discomfort and a sense of insecurity about the proceedings. When the thumb is tucked inside the fist, the person making this gesture is preparing themselves to confront a perceived threat and trying to strengthen themselves, in a completely unconscious way.

Placing the right hand over the heart is a sign that the person you're engaging is asking for your trust and wants to be believed. It's a gesture indicating sincerity. When consciously employed, it can be a ploy to deceive people into believing that the gesturer is sincere, when in fact, they're lying. This gesture is situational, but rooted in a desire to be believed.

Pointing at others is generally considered rude. When the finger is jabbed, this gesture can be read as aggression. Generally, when people point in the course of a conversation, or when delivering a speech, the import is that of authority. The gesture denotes a command of the subject, as well as exhortation and a demand to be heard. Pointing can also provide emphasis (like a form of non-verbal punctuation).

Hands that appear to be squeezing or rubbing each other are a sign of nervousness, or self-pacification. This gesture can be seen in various forms, including lacing and unlacing the fingers, fiddling with rings or cuffs, or picking at the fingernails. The indication is that the gesturer is in a defensive stance and feels threatened or insecure in the context of the interaction.

When people place their hands on their hips, what they're doing physically is taking up more space. By physically magnifying their presence, they're establishing their authority and demanding that they be taken notice of. This is a dominant gesture and when accompanied by planted feet and erect posture, means nothing but business. The person with their hands on their hips (particularly if their hands are in fists) is telling you they are not in a mood for games. This is an "all business" gesture, indicating that the gesturer is uncompromising and not at all open to concessions or negotiations.

Placing the five digits of each hand together, at the fingertips, is called "steepling". While this gesture may easily be misread as conciliatory, what it's really transmitting is that the person making the gesture is inherently confident and authoritative. This is a person who can't be influenced, unless you have an extremely good rationale for whatever it is you're attempting to pitch. The "steepler" is a power player. When you see this hand gesture, you have met someone of considerable intellectual heft who can see through just about anyone.

Facial expressions

The human face is an expressive collection of muscles that can tell you a great deal about people. Even the most apparently inscrutable people speak to others with their faces. In some cultures, this is more the truth than others. Some cultures are even known for a particular ability to conceal the emotions by controlling the face. Most of us, though, wear our emotions and opinions right on our faces, where the whole world can see them.

Most of us are capable of reading facial expressions only rather broadly. We know when someone's happy, because their smile tells us. We know when someone's angry, because the face contorts into an expression that is unpleasant. But there are many expressions the human face is capable of and these can be extraordinarily fleeting, remaining on the face for only from 1/15TH to 1/25TH of a second. That's not a lot of time to get a read. These brief expressions can reveal a lot about what we're thinking (and perhaps don't want to give away with our faces). Known as micro-expressions, there are seven to take note of. These are: contempt, disgust, fear, sadness, surprise, anger and happiness.

These expressions are seen on the faces of people all over the world. They transcend cultural and linguistic boundaries. They are even seen on the faces of those blind from birth and people who have never viewed television or other filmed media. This means that our facial expressions are deeply encoded in our human DNA. They are something we're born knowing how to do, like breathing. Recognizing these is a crucial in the project of learning to understand what people are thinking and feeling. As micro-expressions cross the face so rapidly, knowing the characteristics of each is helpful. Following are the hallmarks of each of the expressions listed:

Disgust: Something stinks! This is the expression your face will form, when that's the case. The nose wrinkles and as it does, the cheeks are pulled upward and the upper lip curls. Lines form under the eyes, as they're narrowed.

Fear: The mouth opens and the lips are drawn back, as both brows rise. As this happens, lines form in the forehead, vertically. The whites of the eyes show, above the iris.

Surprise: The jaw drops, as the mouth opens. The brows shoot up and lines form across the forehead, horizontally. The whites of the eyes show around the full circumference of the iris.

Happiness: As the corners of the mouth turn up, the cheeks rise, the corners of the eyes crease and the lower lids become tense. Teeth may or may not be exposed. Genuine happiness is always indicated when lines form at the outer edges of the eyes. When this doesn't occur, happiness is being feigned.

Anger: As the jaw pushes out, the nostrils dilate. The mouth is tense, with the corners turning down. The brows are pulled together, with vertical lines forming between them. Eyes are fixed. For this expression to be completely readable as anger, all sectors of the face must be engaged.

Contempt: One side of the mouth is raised at the corner in the classical sneer. This expression may be accompanied by the rolling of the eyes.

Sadness: The lower lip is pushed outward and the corners of the mouth, pulled down. The eyebrows are pulled in, then drawn up. Of all the expressions listed in this section, this is the one least likely to be feigned effectively.

These are simple descriptions, but you can practice reproducing them, yourself. Stand in front of the mirror, attempting to match your facial expression to an emotion, without looking at the descriptions above. Now do the same, following the descriptions and paying attention to any differences you note. When you're aware of the subtleties of these expressions on your own face, you'll be more likely to catch them on the faces of others. These expressions can tell you a lot about the quality of a conversation you're having and the level of honesty being shared on the part of the person you're talking to.

Chapter 13 Stop Manipulation

It is believed that being manipulated is limited to a relationship that is shared by two people. This is so not true. Most people can deal with manipulative people and suffer from emotional abuse while dating, after they are married, and don't forget about the people who have been manipulated by their bosses, friends, coworkers, relatives, siblings, and parents. Let's take a close look at these relationships. Let's learn how to identify certain tactics a manipulator might use to gain control over you and discuss some methods that you can use to put an end to their behavior.

Problems You Might Experience

If you are in a manipulative relationship, whether it is with your partner, friends, sibling, or parent, then listen up. Your whole life might be dependent on the manipulator since they don't let you do anything for yourself. They probably control the household finances and make you rely on them for money. If they are your parents they have probably decided for you the subjects you took in school, your career path, whether or not you can have a job, whom you can interact with, and who you are allowed to marry. Some might even tell you what you can eat, say, and wear.

Living in a situation like this can make you feel valueless since you aren't allowed to do anything the way you want to, and will face horrible consequences such as psychological, verbal, and possibly physical abuse if you don't do exactly what they tell you. If you feel as if you don't have control of your life, you will lose interest, and your life will only be something to be endured and not enjoyed. If you aren't allowed to make decisions, your self-confidence will begin to lessen. At the moment when your confidence wanes, you will stop believing in yourself, and any goals you might have set for yourself goes away. You will no longer pursue your ambitions or dreams because your only objective now is to fulfill your manipulator's wishes. With time, your happiness is going to lessen and you will start to teeter on the edge of depression and chronic stress.

There is good news and your life doesn't have to be like this. If you are exhausted from having to live this way, if you want to be free, happy, move on, and permanently end this situation, you have to understand that you aren't to blame for the behavior that they inflict on you. There are actions you can take to put an end to the control your manipulator has over you.

Family

There are many cases where the manipulator was the victim's own guardian, sibling, or parent.

Remember a manipulator loves having power over other people. They assert this power by using subjugating, dominating, and controlling behaviors. They achieve this by using shame, embarrassment, fear, and guilt on their victims. They will manipulate your perceptions and emotions by constantly humiliating you and denial. Once other people begin to see signs of abuse, the manipulator will lie and try to convince them that you are having a mental breakdown. This results in them isolating their victims even more.

Manipulators will prey on people who are very vulnerable like feeble, sick or elderly. They will prey on people who are very needy such as children. In fact, children will suffer from being blamed for situations that they had no control over like being called names, not allowed to have friends, being ignored, being made fun of and criticized, or being forced to do degrading acts.

Manipulators are truly sadistic assassins who get their gratification from making family member fight amongst themselves and engaging in destructive behavior. If you are constantly distracted by family conflicts, then the attention is being drawn away from the true problem; the manipulator.

If your siblings or parents are manipulating you, here are some ways you can identify their behavior:

- They don't let you speak to other people.

- They won't let you express your own views.

- They always decide things for you like your career, life path, and education.

- They humiliate you constantly.

- They make light of your strengths and qualities most of the time in front of others.

- They control your money and won't allow you to have your own bank account even if you are old enough.

- They won't allow you to drive yourself anywhere. They will drop you off where you want to go and will pick you back up at a certain time.

- They will check your phone to see who you have messaged or called.

How to Fight Back:

- Don't engage them.

- Don't play their games.

- Set, tell them, and enforce your boundaries

- Let the manipulator know you have set rules for interacting and engaging with you. You can do this by setting a time frame where you can take a break from the relationship. It might be 30 days or 60 days. That is completely up to you. Tell them this. If they won't respect this, then start the clock over until they learn to respect it.

- Be confident. Let them know you are serious.

- Never feel guilty. This is a way they manipulate you.

- If they don't change their behavior, you might have to look at the relationship again and possibly end it.

- Forgive them and move on with your life. Be open to reconnecting ONLY if they change.

Spouse/Significant Other

There are a lot of women and men who experience emotional abuse within their intimate relationship each year. If you have a relationship with a manipulative person, here are ways you can catch it early in the relationship:

- They will always ask for positive feedback on their qualities and appearance.

- If they see any ways to humiliate you, they will quickly capitalize on it.

- They will constantly share their accomplishments and experiences with you but won't let you talk.

- They will constantly order you around but won't take any requests from you.

- They will use your words against you in a way so others begin to question your recollection and truthfulness.

- They criticize and yell at you. They tell you that you are disrespectful and call you all sorts of names.

- If you don't listen to them, are later than they think you should be when meeting them, or if it takes you longer to do what they wanted you to do, they will get horribly mad at you.

- They will use your insecurities, weaknesses, and vulnerabilities against you to control and hurt you.

If your significant other shows these types of behaviors, you need to take a step back and take a hard look at your relationship with them. You need to end it quickly so you can stop them from manipulating you further.

How to Fight Back:

- Begin with yourself: Know your rights. Figure out what you want from the relationship. Do you really want to leave or stay?

- If necessary, are you willing to leave? You need to be.

- Create a support system and have it in place.

- Get ready for positive and negative outcomes.

- Ask for help if needed.

Boss/Coworkers

Most of the time, bosses and coworkers will try to manipulate you, too. Here are some early signs you need to watch out for so you can spot them:

- Your boss is dictatorial and rude constantly.

- Your cowards figure out your weaknesses and try controlling you by bribing and exploiting you.

- Your boss has never appreciated your work and humiliates you any chance they get.

- Your coworkers treat you as an outsider and crack jokes at your expense.

- Your boss wrongly accuses you of performing poorly and yells at you often.

- Your coworkers spin and twist your words so that it will question your recollection and truthfulness so they can look better than you.

How to Fight Back:

- Never engage with your manipulator.

- Communicate via email to document everything that is said.

- Tell the manipulator that you don't have time to talk and you are busy.

- Stay calm, document everything, and report them to Human Resources.

- Stand up for yourself. Tell them what you will and won't tolerate or accept from them.

- Say, "NO".

Friends

Friends can also be manipulators. They will always get you to open up and reveal your insecurities and most intimate thoughts. They know how it feels to talk with a friend and have somebody listen to you. But be careful. Their real motive will always be to control you. They will use your insecurities and weaknesses to make you feel guilty if you try to resist them. This will leave you hurt and confused.

If any friends try to manipulate you, uses you constantly, abuses you, and is rude to you achieve their wants, they are not your real friends. They are causing emotional abuse. Early signs of manipulation might include:

- Your friends call you humiliating names and make fun of you all the time.

- They get big favors from you and if you don't do exactly what they want, they will threaten to expose your innermost secrets to the world.

- They manipulate you by using your weaknesses against you.

How to Fight Back:

- Become a person that can't be manipulated.

- Say, "NO."

- Set firm boundaries.

Dealing with the Manipulator's Tactics

We are going to look at some of the most common tactics that manipulators will use to get their way and ways to deal with them. Before you deal or confront your abuse you have to be mentally prepared so you don't become frazzled by their manipulative ways. You have to be steel. Never feel sorry for them or get taken by their attempts and tactics when trying to manipulate you. Here is what you need to do when they try to:

- Temper Tantrums

If the manipulator likes to throw tantrums, then you have to deal with them extremely calmly. Remain calm when there are throwing their tantrum. Never react since you don't know if they will become physically violent. After the tantrum is over tell them how this behavior bothers you.

Focus on accomplishing your goals and your work. Show them you don't like being around people who behave this way. You might have to find new friends or a new job. If your friendships aren't positive ones, it is time to make new ones.

- Blaming and Threatening

If your manipulator blames and threatens you, you have to tell them you know what they are trying to do, that it isn't going to work, and you aren't going to take it. Be polite and firm with them but keep constant eye contact with them. Never show weakness. If they try to deny it, let them know you are positive about what you are saying and you aren't allowing the abuse to continue.

Next thing you need to do is set boundaries. Tell them what they can and can't do. How the can and can't act around you and what you will and won't accept from them. Explain the consequences that they are going to face if they continue to treat you like they have been. Tell them they might be facing divorce or separation, you will leave them, and you will report them to Human Resources. If it continues you will get the police involved. If the manipulation continues, you will need to do whatever consequence you warned them about so they will see you mean business.

When you use these tactics, you will be on the right path to end this manipulation. You will be closer to having a healthy life that you richly deserve.

Ways to Stop Being Manipulated

Manipulation happens when a person gets used to benefit another. The person doing the manipulation will deliberately create an imbalance in power and then exploits their victim to serve their own agenda. They will make their victim feel ashamed, guilty, or deprive them of feeling happy if they don't do what was asked of them. This type of abuse is hard to escape. Fortunately, there are ways you can protect yourself from manipulation:

- Know your human rights

The most important guideline when dealing with a manipulative person is knowing your rights and realizing you are being violated. You can defend your rights and stand up for yourself as long as you don't hurt others. If you do bring harm to other people, you have to forfeit these rights. Here is a list of your human rights:

1. You can ask for respect.

2. You can make a healthy and happy life for yourself.

3. You can express your wants, opinions, and feelings.

4. You can protect and take care of yourself from being threatened emotionally, mentally, or physically.

5. You can set your priorities the way you want.

6. Your opinion can be different from other people.

7. You can say, "NO" without feeling guilty.

8. You can get what you pay for.

All these rights are your boundaries.

Society is full of people who have no interest in respecting these rights. Manipulators want to take away your rights so they can take advantage of and control you. You have to moral authority and power to tell the manipulator that you are in charge of your life.

- Never try to be honest with a manipulator

You try to state the truth and it gets turned completely around. Let's say a friend forgot your birthday and you tell them: "I am upset that you didn't remember my birthday." Your friend might respond with: "It upsets me that you would insinuate that I would forget when your birthday is. I should have let you know about all of the stress that I am going through right now, but I didn't want you to worry about me. I should have pushed aside all of my pain to focus on your birthday. I am sorry." Don't be surprised if you see actual tears. Even while you are listening to their words your sneaky suspicion that they aren't actually sorry but because they have said them you have nothing more than you can say. You might find yourself suddenly babysitting their wrath. If you feel like this is the angle they are playing, don't surrender. You don't have to accept this faked apology. If it comes off as insincere, it usually is. Rule one: if you are dealing with a manipulator always trust your gut feeling. Trust in your senses. When a manipulator discovers a maneuver that works, they will add it to their arsenal and you will be fed a diet of nothing but crap.

- Stay away

An easy way to detect a manipulative person is to see if they act differently around various people and situations. We all have a degree of this kind of social differentiation; some manipulators like to dwell in the extremes. They might be completely nice to one person and totally rude to another. They could act completely helpless at times and extremely aggressive at others. When you see this kind of behavior from a person regularly, keep your distance and don't engage with them unless you absolutely have to. The reasons for chronic manipulation are deep-seated and complex. It isn't your job to try and save or change them.

- They act like they are willing to help

If asked for something or to help out, they usually always agree, if they don't volunteer first. Then once you tell them "thanks" they will make a bunch of noise or other signs that tell you they really don't want to actually help out. If you confront them about not wanting to do what they said they would, they will make a big scene by saying "OF COURSE" they were going to help and you are being completely unreasonable. They are just trying to make you feel like you are going crazy. Rule two: if they do tell you "YES" they need to be held accountable for what they agreed to. DON'T buy into all the sighs. If they didn't really want to help out, make them say it, or put on your headphones, take a bath, and then let them live with their drama.

- Stay away from self-blame and personalization

Because their agenda is to find and exploit your weaknesses, you might begin to feel inadequate or start blaming yourself for not being able to satisfy them. With these types of situations, you have to remember that you aren't the problem, you are just being manipulated to feel worthless so you will surrender your rights and power. Think about your relationship with them and ask yourself these questions:

1. Do they treat me with true respect?

2. Do I feel good about myself while in this relationship?

3. Do they have unreasonable demands and expectations of me?

4. Is the giving primarily one or two ways in the relationship?

How you answer these questions will give you important clues as to whether the so-called problem about the relationship is with you or your manipulator.

- Crazy making

This is the manipulator saying something and then later telling you they didn't say it at all. If you are in a position where you think you need to keep a journal of everything that is said since you have begun to question your sanity, you are being manipulated. Manipulators are experts in explaining things away, justifying, rationalizing, and turning things around. They lie very smoothly so you can be sitting and looking at a dog and they will tell you it's a cat. They can argue so persuasively that you will start doubting your own senses. With sometime this will be so eroding and insidious that it can literally change your reality. Being manipulated is extremely dangerous. It will be very unsettling for the manipulator to see you start carrying around a pen and paper and take notes when you talk to them. Tell them you are feeling a bit "forgetful" and you just want to write down what they are saying for posterity. The craziest thing about this is when you have to do this is a big reason why you need to think about removing yourself from the relationship. If you have to take notes just to protect your sanity, your "crap" meter is probably screaming by now.

- Focus on them by asking important questions

Manipulators are going to make demands or requests of you. These offers will make you go to the ends of the world to meet their needs. If you hear an unreasonable request, it might be useful to place the focus on the manipulator by asking them some questions to see if they have any self-awareness to see the injustice of their scheme:

1. "Do you really expect me to...?"

2. "Does this seem reasonable to you?"

3. "What am I getting out of this?"

4. "Does that sound fair to you?"

5. "Are you telling or asking me?"

6. "Do I have any say in this?"

When you ask them these questions, you are making them take a hard look at themselves so that they can see their true nature. If they have any degree of self-awareness, they will likely take back the demand or back down completely.

A true manipulator will just dismiss the questions and insist they get their way. If this happens, use some of the tips given in this chapter to stop the manipulation.

- Manipulators are great guilt mongers

Manipulators will make you feel guilty for not saying something or for saying something, for not caring and giving enough, for caring and giving, for not being emotional enough or being emotional. Everything is open and fair game for a manipulator. They don't express their desires and needs openly. Their only interest is to use manipulation to reach their goals. Guilt isn't the only way but it is the most dangerous one. Many people are conditioned to do what they have to in order to get rid of feelings of guilt. Manipulators also like to use sympathy, which is just as powerful as guilt. Manipulators make the best victims. They show an intense need to be nurtured, cared for, and supported. Manipulators won't fight their own battles or do any of their own dirty work. When you do these things for them, they might just say they didn't expect or want you to do that. Do your best not to fight their battles or doing all of their dirty work for them. One great thing you can tell them is: "I am extremely confident in your ability to figure this out by yourself." Listen carefully to their response and note where the crap meter hits.

Chapter 14 Tips for Safeguarding Yourself from Manipulation

Being a manipulation expert is as much about spotting manipulation and deception in others as it is about leading others to do what you want them to.

Do you want to safeguard yourself from manipulation on a daily basis?

Do you want to prevent people from taking advantage of you for fulfilling their own selfish goals?

Do you want to be able to sniff manipulation from miles away?

Here are 10 brilliant strategies to protect yourself from manipulation.

1. Ignore Their Words and Actions

Manipulators almost always go after shaking people's confidence and making them insecure to get them to do what they (the manipulators) want. They will do their best to plant seeds of apprehension and self-doubt. There is a tendency to make the victim believe that the manipulator's opinion is actually the truth or fact. Rather than wanting to help you, they are more interested in trying to control you.

The best strategy to deal with these negative manipulators is to ignore them rather than trying to argue with them or correct them. This allows them to set an even deeper trap for you. Do not fall for their conflict or confrontation bet. Simply bypass them, without revealing your emotions. Do not let them see the emotions that make you tick. Once they gain a good understanding of your emotional triggers, they will sneakily use it for influencing your thoughts, behavior, and decisions.

Some people are difficult to delete from our life immediately. Think – boss, neighbor, family member, etc. Just pretend to listen to what they are saying, agree with it and eventually do exactly what you want.

2. Do not Compromise

Guilt is one of the most insidious tools used by manipulators to get their victims to do what they want. Of course, it can be used positively to influence a person too, but in negative manipulation, its usage can spell disaster for the victim.

Manipulators induce a feeling of guilt in their victims for their past mistakes, choices, and failures. They will make you guilt about being self-assured and self-confident. Each time you experience happiness, they will make you feel bad about it. Their objective is to never make you feel good about yourself or happy.

They'll sow seeds of self-doubt about your true worth, persona, and abilities. Do not get knocked off balance or feel guilty they start blaming you. Do not doubt your self-worth or abilities. Never believe that you do not deserve happiness or to feel wonderful about yourself. Take pride in who you are and your accomplishments. Build a strong sense of self-esteem and confidence. Do not compromise on your happiness or your feelings about yourself.

3. Do not Fit In, Stand Out

It isn't funny how many people make them susceptible to manipulation by trying hard to fit in. Manipulative people count of your desire to want to fit in to push their agenda. They lead you to believe that everyone does what they want you to do and that those who do not conform are abnormal. That is the only way to control your decisions and behavior.

Give up the notion of trying to fit in, and encourage the idea of standing out among the rest. Be different from other folks. Focus on reinventing yourself, laying your own rules (for what is good for you and others) and avoid cowing down to peer pressure.

4. Stop Seeking Permission

We've been conditioned to ask for permission since childhood, right from when we wanted to be fed as a baby to when we wanted to visit the bathroom in school to waiting for our turn to talk in the boardroom. The result of this conditioning is that people seldom do anything without seeking permission.

There is an excessive focus on being polite and making things comfortable for others. Manipulative people want their victims to live by their own self-drafted, imaginary rules or values. The underlying idea is you are not free to take any decision without consultation. Be brave and give up this sense of confinement. You have the power to change your life without the need to live by someone else's self-fulfilling rules.

5. Do not be a Baby

If you are tricked once, it isn't your fault. However, if you are tricked 15 times, there's something wrong with you. Do not let people take advantage of your by being everyone's favorite punching bag. Have the courage to stand up to manipulators and say a firm no when you know they are taking advantage of you. Stop whining about other people are taking advantage of you, and take complete control of your life.

Victims of manipulation almost always complain about how people use them. No one can take advantage or you without your consent. You are indeed responsible for your own actions and their outcome. If someone has used sneaky tricks to outwit you, it is your fault. Learn from past blunders and stop trusting slippery people again and again. Move away from them. Focus on surrounding yourself with positive, constructive, inspiring and like-minded folks who make you feel good about yourself.

6. Have a Clear Sense of Purpose

When you do not know what you want, you'll be more prone to do whatever everyone else wants. You'll be easily tricked into doing what other people want you to do without a firm goal or objective in life. People who lack a clear purpose or aim tend to function or go through life more mechanically. There is little logic in their actions or decisions. They will be more prone to experiencing a growing sense of emptiness in them that will craftily be filled by a manipulator.

This lack of objective or constructive activities makes the manipulator feel empowered enough to easily distract you or draw you to their agenda.

Have a higher purpose in life. It can be anything from taking up a cause for the betterment of the community to traveling around the world to rising in your professional life. Do not allow manipulators an opportunity to prey on your sense of purposelessness. When you are absolutely clear about where you are headed, it is difficult to stop you or get you to change tracks.

Conclusion

Thank for making it through to the end of Manipulation.

Manipulation is being used in every area of life; from TV to advertisements. While some forms might not be as cynical as others, manipulation in relationships and inter-personal relationships cause more problems than one might think. Equipped with the right tools, you can now spot manipulation and put an end to it before it harms you.

Since manipulation is so prevalent in our world, it's hard to avoid it altogether. But, keeping an eye and ear out can help you find those in your life that are more interested in their own needs and using you to get there.

Remember, don't allow yourself to stoop to their level. The best payback is to show them that you can live your own life without their influence. Burst their bubble when you see right through their manipulation tactics. That hurts them the most when they can't manipulate you to get what they want.